RUNNING
ON·EMPTY

· ELLEN SUE STERN ·

Running

ON · EMPTY

Meditations for
Indispensable Women

BANTAM BOOKS
NEW YORK · TORONTO
LONDON · SYDNEY · AUCKLAND

RUNNING ON EMPTY

A Bantam Book/February 1992

See page 375 for acknowledgments.

Library of Congress Cataloging-in-Publication Data

Stern, Ellen Sue
    Running on empty : meditations for indispensable
women / Ellen Sue Stern.
        p.   cm.
    ISBN 0-553-35149-4
    1. Women—Prayer-books and devotions—English.
    I. Title.
        II. Title: Indispensable women.
        BL625.7.S74   1992   91-34060
        305.4—dc20   CIP

Published simultaneously in the United States and Canada

Bantam Books are published by Bantam Books, a division of Bantam
Doubleday Dell Publishing Group, Inc. Its trademark, consisting of the
words "Bantam Books" and the portrayal of a rooster, is Registered in U.S.
Patent and Trademark Office and in other countries. Marca Registrada.
Bantam Books, 666 Fifth Avenue, New York, New York 10103.

PRINTED IN THE UNITED STATES OF AMERICA

FFG   0 9 8 7 6 5 4 3 2 1

For my parents,
Frank and Rosalie Kiperstin,
With love and gratitude

ACKNOWLEDGMENTS

This book was written during a particularly challenging time in my life. I needed lots of support—and I wish to thank my family and friends who helped keep me confident and on track.

I wish to pay special tribute to the following individuals:

Jill Edelstein: for your love, humor, and patience. I am infinitely grateful.

Gary Stern: for your wonderful editing of the manuscript.

Martha Morris: for your friendship and optimism throughout.

Beverly Lewis and Joseph Pittman: for terrific editorial support and dedication to this project.

Rebecca Rising: for your wonderful help in supplying quotes.

Joseph Morris: for giving me so much joy.

It's easier to do it myself.

—The Indispensable Woman

It's the battle cry of women everywhere. And to a point, truer words were never spoken. It *is* easier to do it all yourself than to wait for someone else to do it or teach them how to do it or forgive them when they don't do it *right*. But in the long run, taking on too much responsibility wears you out until you're like a dying battery.

As we begin the New Year, know that letting go of some of our responsibility frees us to focus on what's truly important. Begin the process of recovery by repeating these words:

❄ AFFIRMATION:
I will carefully choose how I expend my energy.

RUSHING

Oh dear! Oh dear! I shall be too late!

—The White Rabbit (Lewis Carroll)

Running, running, running like the rabbit in *Alice in Wonderland*. But what's the rush?

In our frantic drive to get there, we forget where we're going. Each day is one long race with ourselves, but there's no way to win. We can't savor the joy of being alive when we're perpetually running.

We need to slow down and take our time. We deserve to enjoy life, not just hurry through it.

AFFIRMATION:

If it's really important, I can take my time and do it right.

Keep two truths in your pocket and take each one out according to your need. Let one be: For my sake was the world created. Let the other be: I am nothing but dust and ashes.

—*Hasidic proverb*

Balance comes from allowing ourselves simply to be human—neither grandiose nor self-deprecating, neither in charge of fixing everything nor incapable of doing anything right.

It is such a relief to stop trying to make ourselves indispensable, to no longer feel as if the world will stop spinning if we let go.

The universe continues to unfold without our holding it in our hands.

❀ AFFIRMATION:
I belong here along with every living creature.

ABUNDANCE

Everything is either love or fear. Whatever isn't love is fear. Whatever isn't fear is love.

—A Course in Miracles

Not enough time. Not enough energy. Not enough love.

Fear rules our lives; a scarcity mentality keeps us pushing and pressuring ourselves until we're ready to drop.

Making ourselves crazy won't help us accomplish more. On the contrary, productivity soars when we're relaxed and secure. Instead of being ragged and anxious, we are aware of clear, clean energy flowing through us when we love ourselves and trust that the universe is supporting us.

AFFIRMATION:
I have everything I need.

Pretty is as pretty does.

—*Common saying*

Wherever I travel, Indispensable Women report that this saying rings in their ears. The message is: Inner beauty is based on outward accomplishment.

No matter how enlightened parents are, all of us are raised with some measure of conditional love. Consequently we feel that we have to perform and produce in order to be loved, in order to be accepted.

True beauty comes from our essence, not our effort. We value the people we love for who they are, not because they have a great job or make fabulous crepes suzette.

It's time to extend the same respect to ourselves.

✿ AFFIRMATION:
I am not my accomplishments.

> *Women are the glue that holds our day-to-day life together.*
>
> —*Anna Quindlen*

Women are incredible! We love with abandon; we give as if there were no tomorrow.

Sometimes we give until we've given ourselves away. We become drained and exhausted. We start out inspired and end up resentful.

How are such noble intentions thwarted? Something important is missing—our ability to value ourselves at least as much as we value others.

Putting ourselves first is *not* selfish. It is a necessary discipline in order to consciously channel our energies, stay focused, and keep going.

❊ AFFIRMATION:
I can only give when I am nourished and rested.

And on the seventh day, God rested.

—*Genesis* 2:2

We get sick in order to remove ourselves from the rat race, crawl under the covers, and fall into the depths of blessed sleep. We are *so* worn out, yet we refuse to build rest and relaxation into our lives.

True "R and R" is essential if we are to realize our potential without compromising our health. Downtime replenishes creativity.

If we can't stop running, we may be running away from something. It takes courage to be quiet, to listen to the still voice within.

AFFIRMATION:
Every day I will find fifteen minutes for rest and contemplation.

We approach life as if it were an assignment, with a good report card the reward.

—The Indispensable Woman

Everything feels like a task and a test to Indispensable Women. Like schoolchildren terrified of the teacher, we tense up and worry, worry, worry about whether we will pass.

But we're grading on the wrong scale. Instead of giving ourselves A's for achievement and F's for failure, we need to award ourselves gold stars for doing our best and yes, for enjoying our lives.

Life is its own reward. When we focus on the end goal, on the product rather than the process, we miss out on the best part of life—living.

AFFIRMATION:
I am in charge of my own life. I will decide what is good enough.

If we did not worry, most of us would feel that we were not alive.

—*J. Krishnamurti*

Worrying about problems and solving them consumes Indispensable Women, making us feel challenged, exhilarated, and important.

But what if, for just one day, there was nothing to worry about? Nothing to fix? If we could enjoy life without solving anything or rescuing anybody?

The drama of worrying distracts us from experiencing deeper feelings of sadness and yearning. It keeps us in our heads instead of our hearts.

 **AFFIRMATION:**
My life is too precious to waste it worrying.

> *"Why are you selling those?"* asked the little prince.
>
> *"Because they save a tremendous amount of time,"* said the merchant. *"Computations have been made by experts. With these pills, you save fifty-three minutes every week."*
>
> *"And what do I do with those fifty-three minutes?"*
>
> *"Anything you like. . . ."*
>
> *"As for me,"* said the little prince to himself, *"if I had fifty-three minutes to spend as I liked, I should walk at my leisure toward a spring of fresh water."*
>
> —Antoine de Saint-Exupery, The Little Prince

What good is fifteen minutes saved when we've spent it worrying? A woman in one of my Indispensable Woman workshops told this story: One night she was rushing to get dinner on the table. Her children, four and six, begged to help make the spaghetti. "No," she said, frazzled and panic-stricken, envisioning puddles of spaghetti sauce all over the floor. Then she caught herself and changed her mind. Together they twirled spaghetti, laughing and making alphabet letters and stick figures, having a wonderful time.

Close your eyes and get in touch with the three most important things in your life. Are you making time for them? If not, start now.

✿ AFFIRMATION:
Today I will choose an activity and proceed slowly, taking time to appreciate the experience.

Relationships are where we take our recovery show on the road.

—*Melody Beattie*

Indispensability is a way of avoiding intimacy. And it works! We're so competent, we appear not to need other people's support and affection.

We forget that part of loving is allowing others to give too. We push away those we love, barricaded behind all-important responsibilities that take precedence over everything else. We're too busy to feel, and that makes intimacy impossible.

But indispensability is no substitute for love. It turns us into robots, leaving us lonely and cold. Intimacy requires softness, acknowledging our need for another person. It is a risk worth taking.

❀ AFFIRMATION:
If people really knew me, they'd know how terrific I am.

Who is the modern woman? She faints not, neither does she grow melancholy. Her price is far above rubies. She keeps on running.

—Norma Rosen

In the Jewish tradition, when we want to praise or eulogize a woman, we call her a Woman of Valor.

Whatever our particular religious training, we most likely learned that a "good woman" gives and gives, often without regard for her own needs. Sacrifice equals holiness.

Perhaps we should redefine what it means to be a jewel among women, juggling the incredible demands of contemporary life. Let's give medals to Indispensable Women who give themselves a mental health day, who care enough about themselves to stop running.

❈ AFFIRMATION:
I sparkle more brightly when I am rested.

> *Lying on her deathbed, the codependent woman sees some-*
> *one else's life flash before her eyes.*
>
> —*Anonymous*

Lying on *her* deathbed, the Indispensable Woman makes a seating chart for the funeral.

Crazy as it sounds, with our last breath we would still allow other people's needs and concerns to eclipse our own. Diverting our focus to other people allows us to feel needed *and* gives us the perfect excuse to avoid the pain and growth that comes from dealing with our own issues.

But our own lives need to be our absolute first priority. We can play a part in other people's lives, but it costs us dearly when we take over as director, cast, and crew.

❀ AFFIRMATION:
I am responsible for me. They are responsible for themselves.

When you are sad, learn something.

—Merlin

When I'm sad, I snap into action. Suddenly I'm washing the kitchen floor or returning business calls or finishing an article I've long been avoiding.

It's easier to immerse ourselves in activity than to feel our sadness. Yet sadness is a great gift. It's an opportunity for going deeper and discovering new truths about ourselves. Sadness gives us important information about what we yearn for, what we need in order to be more peaceful and fulfilled.

❈ AFFIRMATION:
I welcome my sadness and trust myself to feel only as much as I can afford to.

She nurses a fantasy of escaping to a desert island, where no one, no one, expects anything of her. But to the world, she looks as if she expects to be named "Woman of the Year."
        —The Indispensable Woman

Our insides and outsides don't match. Inside we are tired, drained, and resentful of how much everyone expects of us. Outside we appear to be handling it all perfectly.

As long as we foster an image of infallibility, we continue to dig our own grave. If no one knows we need help, no one will offer to help us.

It's scary to let down our guard, to appear average instead of extraordinary, even for a moment. Yet, you'd be amazed at how loving and supportive others can be when we share our real feelings, including our fatigue.

✿ AFFIRMATION:
I don't have to escape to a desert island in order to take a break.

I know who I am by looking at my list.

—Karen T.

We define ourselves on the basis of our responsibilities. Our very identities depend on those creased scraps of paper at the bottom of the purse.

Making our list, reading our list, crossing off a couple of "dones" on our list gives us a great feeling of control. "I've got a handle on it now," we say to ourselves, heaving a great sigh of relief, or, "Look at all I have to do. I *must* be important!"

Lists are great for being organized, as long as we don't allow ourselves to be hostage to them. They are meant to act as an assistant, not a slave driver.

❁ AFFIRMATION:
I know who I am by looking inside myself.

Willfulness must give way to willingness and surrender.
Mastery must yield to mystery.

—Gerald G. May

We try to direct the course of our destiny, thinking we have the ability to choreograph every step in order to make life turn out just right.

The real trick is to let go and be receptive. Surrendering means suspending our disbelief with a willing and open heart. It means remaining alert to every opportunity with perfect trust that the next step will reveal itself in time.

❇ AFFIRMATION:
Life is a magnificent journey with interesting twists and turns. I can veer off course without losing my way.

And I'm working all day and I'm working all night
To be good-looking, healthy, and wise.
And adored.
And contented.
And brave.
And well-read.
And a marvelous hostess,
Fantastic in bed,
And bilingual,
Athletic,
Artistic . . .
Won't someone please stop me?

—Judith Viorst

It isn't enough for Indispensable Women to do well at one thing—or even a couple of things. As soon as we master one arena, we go on to the next. We get a promotion—we'd better get the new kitchen wallpaper up. Our hair is finally the right color—it's time to learn to make sushi. It's exhausting to push ourselves so hard. And for what? To impress other people? To get the love we need?

The compulsion to be superaccomplished comes out of deep insecurity. But no amount of achievement will ever be enough to make us feel loved. Loving ourselves comes from accepting our gifts *and* our limitations.

❄ AFFIRMATION:
The only good reason to take something on is because I truly want to do it.

I say no and then I call back and say, "I'm sorry, I meant yes."

—*I.W. (Indispensable Woman)*
workshop participant

We get scared and we capitulate. Saying no feels risky; we're afraid other people will get mad or withdraw their friendship if we don't deliver.

Healthy relationships require firm boundaries. And firm boundaries can only be asserted by individuals with a firm sense of self.

When we value our time, energy, and abilities, we make conscious choices. We say yes some of the time and no some of the time. Being discriminating is far better than being a doormat.

Saying no takes practice. One trick is to never commit on the spot. Say, "I'll call you back," or "Let me think about it." If we put a premium on ourselves, others treat us accordingly.

✳ **AFFIRMATION:**
I've learned to say yes. I can learn to say no.

Where others find love and contentment,
we still often have to strive
to remember we are worthy
and heroes just to be alive.

—Elia Wise

Life is a struggle for everyone recovering from abusive childhoods. Regardless of who we are as adults, the child within cries out for reassurance and love, to be told again and again that it wasn't our fault, that to have survived is indeed a worthy and heroic act.

I was very moved by a passage from Elia Wise's beautiful little book, *For Children Who Were Broken.* It reminds me that indispensability is a survival mechanism. It is how we cope in order to anesthetize our pain.

But the child within needs to be comforted. So does the adult. Be very gentle with yourself and notice how far you've come.

❀ AFFIRMATION:
Every day I am healing a little bit more.

A mind that is fast is sick.
A mind that is slow is sound.
A mind that is still is divine.

—*Meher Baba*

Thinking fast—partly because we have so much to think about, partly because we have to stay ahead of the game—keeps us from thinking well.

Our minds become cluttered and disoriented; we can only afford to give the most superficial attention.

When we take time to slow down our process and really sort things out, we make wise and informed choices. We can see all the angles.

And when our minds are still, in a meditative state, knowledge flows through us effortlessly. It no longer hurts to think.

AFFIRMATION:
I know more than I know.

What's the opposite of an Indispensable Woman? A Dispensable Woman? A Disposable Woman?

—The Indispensable Woman

We function as if we have only two speeds—On or Off. High-speed performance or total collapse with nothing in between.

Fear of being ordinary keeps us entrenched in our indispensability. If we say no to our children, will they stop needing us? If we cut back our schedules, will we be left with nothing to do, facing a terrifying void?

The opposite of an Indispensable Woman is a human being. Nothing more, and not a bit less.

AFFIRMATION:

I can moderate my activity without losing my worth.

The fact that your spouse isn't perfect shouldn't be your problem. If your husband or wife were perfect, then you wouldn't need any talent or wisdom.

—*Rabbi Manis Friedman*

When perfection is the standard, no one measures up. Your mate, friends, and children can't help but disappoint you, and eventually they recoil from your constant barrage of criticism.

In the twelve-step-recovery world there is a saying: "Don't take anyone else's inventory." It means, stop focusing on other people's issues and concentrate on your own.

For one thing, we only have control over ourselves. For another, as Rabbi Friedman points out, the much greater challenge is to call upon our best selves to love and accept others, in all their imperfection.

Isn't that how we want to be loved?

❀ AFFIRMATION:
I can allow other people their flaws. It's part of what makes them lovable.

When I turned thirty, I devised a kind of five-year plan. I figured that by thirty-five—if not now, when?—I would have resolved nine out of ten personal problems. It never occurred to me that I would get any more.

—Ellen Goodman

Indispensable Women thrive on deadlines. Five-year plans. Ten-year plans. They make us feel as though we know where we're going and how to get there.

Once we get "there," there's somewhere new to go. There's always another problem to solve. Another challenge to meet. Getting older doesn't mean the problems go away; we simply become more confident. We don't panic; we know we have the necessary tools.

❈ **AFFIRMATION:**
Death is the only real deadline. As long as I'm alive, there's more to learn.

> *You aren't responsible for anything that happened to you*
> *as a child. You are responsible for everything you do as an*
> *adult.*

> —Susan Forward

Blaming our parents is vastly different from owning what really happened when we were little. Blame keeps us victimized; truth frees us to live our lives with confidence and serenity.

Remembering our hurt and learning how it shaped us is good, solid information. It informs us of our fragility and teaches us what we need in order to heal. But confronting our parents isn't essential for healing; it won't necessarily help and can add more salt to our wounds.

The point is to acknowledge what happened—in a safe place, with a therapist or trusted friend—and then go about the adult business of living our lives. We can ease this process by surrounding ourselves with friends who shower us with unconditional love.

❈ AFFIRMATION:
I will never again allow anyone to abuse me.

Our lives are both ordinary and mythical. We live and die, age beautifully or full of wrinkles. We wake in the morning, buy yellow cheese, and hope we have enough money to pay for it. At the same instant we have these magnificent hearts that pump through all sorrow and all winters we are alive on the earth.

—Natalie Goldberg

The paradox is that each and every one of us is, in fact, indispensable. Our lives matter; each of us has a vital role to play.

We create drama because we don't believe, in our hearts, that our lives are big enough, important enough. We forget that at every moment we have the power to make a difference. When we smile at a stranger on a bus, tuck a sleepy child in bed, or illuminate other people's experience with a fresh insight, we matter.

Every day is ripe with instances of holiness. All we need to do is wake up in the morning and open our eyes.

❄ AFFIRMATION:
I matter.

There's no such thing as a mother who doesn't work.
                                        —*Anonymous*

I often ask an audience of women to raise their hands if they work. Hands of "career women" shoot up, while the remaining women hold theirs in their laps, looking uncomfortable or embarrassed.

All women work. Anytime we expend energy doing anything for anybody, we work. Whether we cook dinner, run a company, or volunteer to be Room Mother, whether we get paid in love, money, or self-satisfaction, we work.

It's critical to put a value on our time and energy. Otherwise we sell ourselves short.

❄ AFFIRMATION:
I am not expendable. Everything I do has inherent value.

Why would I want to have everything? Where would I put it?

—A comic

Laughter is the best way I know to put things in perspective. When we take a step back, we see the big picture; we can sort out what's real and what we've bought into, perhaps without even realizing it.

In the 1970s and 1980s, women were sold a bill of goods. The myth of having it all—personified by Superwoman (who finally dropped dead of exhaustion)—is exactly that, a myth. We believed that if we just set our sights higher and worked harder, faster, and smarter, we could make it all happen.

But real life is a series of endless compromises. There isn't a way to have everything. There *is* a way to achieve some measure of peace if we make choices based on our most deeply held values.

❋ **AFFIRMATION:**
I only have room in my life for what's truly important.

It's time to stop making lists and start making love.
                              —The Indispensable Woman

Sex is one of the first things to go when we get caught in the cycle of indispensability. Often it doesn't even make the list of what's important in our lives.

We become cold and unapproachable. We don't have time to be close and let ourselves be loved. After a while, we don't even miss it.

Making love makes us soft. And vulnerable. And more real. It takes us out of our heads and into our bodies. At the very least, sex is an important antidote to the loneliness of our indispensability. At its best, sex brings us closer to ourselves, to our infinite capacity for love and spiritual connection.

❈ AFFIRMATION:
My sexuality is a glorious gift to open whenever I choose.

Angels can do no better.

—*K. Panuthos*

When I start pressuring myself, I try to remember this simple truth I read many years ago in a lovely book called *Transformation Through Birth.* Although the author was referring to childbirth, I repeat the words to myself whenever I feel insecure.

Expectations are our worst enemies. We set unreachable goals and inevitably fall short and then feel bad about ourselves.

No one but you expects you to be perfect. Instead, try being a really good friend to yourself. Good friends praise us when we do well and comfort us when we miss the mark. But they never stop loving us.

✿ AFFIRMATION:
My best is the best I can do.

> *To everything there is a season, and a time for every*
> *purpose under heaven.*
> —*Ecclesiastes* 3:2

It is such a relief to stop being controlled by the master schedule. There is no schedule. There is only putting one foot in front of the other and trusting that we will not fall down. And if we do fall down, we get to see the world from a whole new vantage point.

The best things happen when we least expect them, when they're not on the agenda. We trade the illusion of control for the element of surprise.

Everything occurs in its own time. Exactly as it should. The Yiddish word for this is *b-sheret*, which means "as it is destined."

❀ AFFIRMATION:
There is plenty of time.

Wherever you go, there you are.

—Al-Anon

We can worry all the way there, plotting and schem-
ing. Or we can move with a sure heart. Either way, we
end up in the same place.

Often I live by a schedule, and if I'm really
overcommitted, I even break it up into fifteen-minute
increments. Then I follow it religiously. Every minute
is accounted for; I break into a sweat if I fall behind,
terrified I won't make the finish line.

But once in a while, even when I'm at my busiest, I
throw caution to the wind and toss the Holy Schedule aside. I take the long way home around the lakes.
Or spontaneously meet a friend for lunch. I always
end up with twice the energy.

❈ AFFIRMATION:
Everything that happens leads me somewhere.

Don't eat more than you can lift.

—Miss Piggy

My seven-year-old son, Evan, says this means: Don't stuff yourself.

I agree. We're so hungry for experience, we grab life with both hands and swallow it whole.

It's better to eat a little less and taste a little more. To enjoy the full benefit, we need to slow down enough to digest our experiences.

Again, it's fear that propels us. Fear that if we don't fill our plate to overflowing, all the food will be gone. So we eat until we're sick instead of eating until we're full.

❉ AFFIRMATION:
Nobody is going to remove my plate until I am finished.

Q. *Do you look more together than you feel?*
A. *I hope so.*

—*Dialogue at an I.W. Seminar*

Like most Indispensable Women, I come across as if I have my act together. I know how to present myself so that other people are impressed. Occasionally I even impress myself.

But if you looked inside my purse, you'd see the other side. My purse is the garbage pit of my psyche; it represents the chaos and confusion lurking beneath my polished veneer.

Whenever I'm leaving on a trip, I clean out my purse. It makes me feel as if I'm starting out in an orderly fashion. But soon it fills back up, my secret refuge from the constant strain of keeping up a good front.

✿ AFFIRMATION:
It's okay to look together when I'm falling apart, as long as I'm not fooling myself.

Don't sweat the small stuff.
It's all small stuff.

—*Popular poster*

We wear ourselves out because we can't discriminate between what's urgent and what's not, what's worth getting upset over and what's no big deal.

Everything seems big. In truth, there are few actual emergencies; everything else is the normal stuff of life.

Recovery Lesson #1 for Indispensable Women: PRI-ORITIZE. What can wait? What can be delegated? What can be left undone? If you're not sure, close your eyes and take a moment to answer this question: What is the most important thing in life to me?

Now decide what's worth sweating over.

❀ AFFIRMATION:
If I know what's important, my day-to-day priorities will fall into place.

We're brilliant when it comes to figuring out other people's needs.

—The Indispensable Woman

Anticipating other people's needs and coming up with ways to fulfill them is how Indispensable Women get love. Meanwhile, we're so caught up in taking care of everybody else, we haven't the time or the wherewithal to take care of ourselves.

Most of the time we don't even notice that we have stopped eating right, aren't exercising, or skipped that mental health day we desperately need.

The fact is, if we don't attend to our own needs, we won't have anything left to give. We need to tune in and take *ourselves* seriously.

AFFIRMATION:

It's about time I paid attention to my needs.

> *Show me a woman who doesn't feel guilty and I'll show you a man.*
>
> —Rachel Hare-Mustin

Whenever I speak to an audience of women, no matter what group I am addressing, someone inevitably asks if *they* are the most guilty. Jewish women assume they feel the guiltiest. Catholic women are convinced they win the prize. Teachers, managers, mothers with careers—all believe they have the market cornered on guilt.

On some level our guilt is proof that we care, that we haven't abandoned our child, or our boss, or the aging parent we don't see often enough because we don't have the time or resources to travel halfway across the country.

Guilt is the next best thing to being there. But it's a poor substitute for being at peace with where we are.

❧ AFFIRMATION:
I can be good without being guilty.

> *Waiting is not mere empty hoping. It has the inner certainty of reaching the goal.*

—I Ching

Indispensable Women think that waiting equals wasting time.

How nice to have permission to wait peacefully.

Consider the expectant mother as she waits for her baby's arrival. Nothing she does makes the time move faster. Meanwhile, her baby grows eyelashes and fingernails.

To allow ourselves to wait calmly is to give ourselves an enormous gift. It is the gift of confidence.

❀ AFFIRMATION:
I am willing to wait.

Q. *How are you?*
A. *I'm as good as my last phone call.*

—Mossie R.

When I asked the mother of a friend how she was doing, that was her response.

A self-described recovering codependent, this woman, whose grown child lives half-way across the country, still determines her own happiness by the sound of her daughter's voice. If her daughter is having a good day, she's happy. If something's wrong, she worries—and wonders if there's something *she* might have done differently.

We can care deeply about other people. We can hurt for their pain and rejoice in their happiness. But when *their* state of mind has the power to make or break *our* day, something's wrong. It means we're way too involved in other peoples' lives, and not invested enough in our own.

❀ AFFIRMATION:
Nobody else makes me happy. Nobody else makes me sad.

If the only prayer you say in your whole life is "Thank you," that would suffice.

—Meister Eckhart

Be sure to express gratitude, whether it's thanking your child for picking a dandelion or thanking God for putting it there in the first place.

Saying thank you for all the abundance in our lives —including the tough stuff—is essential to recovery from indispensability. It helps us remember that the universe holds wonders far beyond the seemingly urgent details of our lives.

❋ AFFIRMATION:
I am so lucky to be alive.

Your son is your son till he takes him a wife. Your daughter's your daughter the rest of your life.

—*Common saying*

This was one of my Grandma Sophie's favorite quotes. Lucky for her, she had three daughters!

Women have been brought up as primary caretakers in our families. We expect more from ourselves than from our brothers. When our parents age and become dependent, we naturally feel responsible for their care, even if we are already overextended with career, marriage, and mothering.

As children we sometimes took on more than we could handle so we wouldn't disappoint our parents. And we still fear losing their love and approval. But just as we once had to share our parents' attention with our siblings, we now get to share the responsibility.

❋ AFFIRMATION:
If I'm an only child, I need to seek other support for my parents. If I'm not an only child, why am I acting like one?

What a wonderful life I've had! I only wish I'd realized it sooner!

—Colette

Often it takes something startling to remind us how truly blessed we are. A dear friend becomes ill—or dies—and we are catapulted into taking stock. An April blizzard turns everything sparkling white; we open the front door and burst out laughing even though it's just another Thursday and the mortgage is due by the end of the week.

These are powerful messages that tell us how precious life is. They are all around.

✿ AFFIRMATION:
Today I will live life in the present.

At first there is a sense of exhilaration, your adrenaline races with the drama of trying to coordinate it all.

—The Indispensable Woman

Being indispensable is a rush. We get high on the excitement and hooked on the intensity.

Women who do too much do it because of the payoffs. As in any addictive process, we build up a tolerance. The more we do, the more we have to do in order to get high.

What's the difference between doing our best and doing too much? There's less pleasure and more pain. We know we're making ourselves indispensable when it hurts but we can't stop.

AFFIRMATION:

I will pay attention to what I get out of making myself indispensable.

*In my own mind, I am still that fat brunette from Toledo,
and I will always be.*

—Gloria Steinem

We look in the mirror, face a chubby adolescent with
zits and the wrong clothes, and all our adult confidence flies right out the window.

We invest enormous energy trying to look good so
we'll like ourselves. "It takes forty-five minutes to
dress and put my makeup on to run down to the store
and buy a bottle of milk," says a beautifully groomed
woman.

Think about the time we waste! Think about how
hard it is to love ourselves!

❊ AFFIRMATION:
I am beautiful.

To wake at dawn with a winged heart and give thanks for another day of loving.

—*Kahlil Gibran*

Valentine's Day—a day for love. A day when we're particularly aware of our romantic relationships.

If you're part of a couple, you may feel especially pressured today to choose the perfect card or gift to express your sentiments. Keep it simple, and remember that your love is the perfect gift.

Any holiday, but especially Valentine's Day, is painful if we're not in an intimate relationship. It's easy to feel insecure and sorry for ourselves.

Know there will be romance in your life if you want it. When you're ready. Meanwhile, call one person you care about and say, "I love you."

❀ AFFIRMATION:
I am ready to love and be loved.

> *Every encounter demands too much, tears the nerves, drains the will, and the specter of something as small as an unanswered letter arouses such disproportionate guilt that answering it becomes out of the question.*
>
> —Joan Didion

We paralyze ourselves with perfectionism. Nothing we do can possibly meet our expectations. So why try?

The only way to break this pattern is to begin. Do *something!* Make an effort. Even if the result falls short of what you're capable of, it will get you off and running.

My favorite teacher in grade school always complimented us for trying. *Try.* That's all you should expect of yourself.

❋ AFFIRMATION:
I only have to do one thing at a time.

No one can make you feel inferior without your consent.
—*Eleanor Roosevelt*

Wow! We really *do* give other people an awful lot of power!

When we feel bad about ourselves, nothing anyone says or does can change our mind. "You're wrong!" we shoot back. "Take another look and you'll see!"

We give up our good feelings without so much as a whimper. The mere suggestion that anything is wrong with us sends us spiraling into a black hole of self-doubt.

Why should we let anyone diminish our self-esteem? We've fought way too hard to have it!

✿ AFFIRMATION:
I won't allow anyone, under any circumstances, to shake my self-confidence.

Definition of "guts": *Grace under pressure.*
                    —*Ernest Hemingway in* The New Yorker

My image of grace under pressure was indelibly imprinted at nine years old, when I was mesmerized by
the sight of Jacqueline Kennedy as she stood before
President Kennedy's coffin, holding her children's
hands.

Over the years I've collected other role models of
grace under pressure: my friends Jeff and Jan mourning their son Logan's death, my own mother braving
chemotherapy with optimism and humor.

It's good to have powerful images to call upon
in difficult times, to know, when we feel as if we're
falling apart, that we can take a deep breath, gather
ourselves, and find the courage to remain calm and
self-possessed.

❋ AFFIRMATION:
I will get through it.

How desirable and how distant is the ideal of the contemplative, artist, or saint—the inviolable core, the single eye.
                                        —Anne Morrow Lindbergh

Oh, to have the luxury of contemplative time! To pour every ounce of energy into creating beautiful things. To train our eye on one—*one*—goal at a time. To give freely without being torn in a thousand directions; to live without apology for what's left undone.

This is true freedom. It's what women yearn for and rarely find. Sparks of inspiration are buried under deadlines and dirty laundry. We're too tired at the end of the day to paint the picture or write the poem that danced through our mid-morning daydreams.

The first step: buy a journal (a notebook will do) and promise to write for ten minutes every day. Do it when you're alone, even if it means locking yourself in the bathroom. Do it religiously.

❋ AFFIRMATION:
Today I will begin to express my creativity.

Affirmations? That's when you lie to yourself until it's true.

—Linda Maakes

Sometimes we fake it until we're all the way there. We tell ourselves "I can do it" or "Everything will be fine," hoping against hope that it's true.

Maybe we're not sure we can do it. Maybe we're scared to death that everything won't turn out all right.

That's okay. We can—and must—still put out for what we want. The more we trust in our capacity to create joy and abundance, the more we square our shoulders and apply our best energy, the better chance we have of getting what we want.

❊ AFFIRMATION:
I can have doubts and still be positive.

Life is but an endless series of experiments.

—*Mahatma Gandhi*

It's best to conduct an experiment with an open mind, curious to see what will happen, not knowing the results ahead of time. If we don't like how it turns out, we can try something different.

Remember being a kid and mixing food coloring in a jar? Anything could happen, especially if you threw in confetti and some chocolate chips.

We can live this way—inquisitively, without attachment to a specific outcome. When we're set on the end result, we narrow our vision and are easily disappointed. When we experiment, we feel wonder and amazement.

❊ AFFIRMATION:
I can start over as many times as I want.

Why hadn't I made sure to be there on time? Why hadn't I told Yemi to be in at nine so that I could dress without any pressure. . . . I was giving myself bad marks all around.
                                                        —Barbara J. Berg

We're so hard on ourselves. When something goes wrong, we grab the blame, turning our failure over and over like a dog with a bone, until we've gnawed our self-esteem down to nothing.

Being indispensable means we should be able to prevent anything from ever going wrong. Right? *Wrong!* Sometimes things just happen. Without any help from us. We have to give up the illusion of control and give ourselves a break!

❄ AFFIRMATION:
I make mistakes. So what?

It is striking that for woman, any break or separation carries with it an aura of loss, as if the symbolic umbilical cord still affected all her emotional life and each act were a threat to unity and ties.

—Anaïs Nin

Making ourselves indispensable is a way of making sure other people need us. Whether it's parting from a lover or watching our children leave the nest, we hang on long after it makes sense.

We're dependent on *their* dependency. When we let go, we feel lost and helpless. The primal terror of abandonment is reenacted again and again.

We will do almost anything to avoid being left. But there is nothing to do, which is the hardest thing for Indispensable Women to face.

�֎ AFFIRMATION:
Every person is a single person.

Divinity is aimed at humanity.

—Hildegard of Bingen

We work overtime deciphering the divine plan when it's right in front of us as plain as can be.

We are human. We are divine. When we reach with the highest part of ourselves, we can almost touch heaven. When we stumble, the glorious sunset spreads through the sky just the same. In between we ponder what we're doing here.

�֎ **AFFIRMATION:**
I'm doing fine. If there's something more or different I should be doing, it will be revealed.

My response to any physical or psychological assault was to grit it out, marching blindly and bravely into the next ambush.

—Mary Kay Blakely

Many times I have forced myself to grind out work in spite of a blinding migraine headache, instead of climbing under the covers where I belong.

We don't know when to stop! Recently I watched with horror as CNN newscasters in Tel Aviv fumbled with gas masks while giving updates on the war in the Gulf. Meanwhile sirens blared in the background. Would they get the masks on in time?

No one is going to present us with a Purple Heart for pushing through until we collapse. It's *our* responsibility to monitor our pace and know when enough is enough.

❋ AFFIRMATION:
I will make a point of noticing how my body feels and respect its limits.

Let go, let us.

—*Judy F.*

Last year I spent a week with a wonderful group of women—labor nurses, midwives, and childbirth educators—certifying them to lead my Expecting Change Workshops for pregnant women. After six years of running the workshops myself, I had to trust someone else to take over. It was like seeing my baby off to college, hoping and praying she would survive the first semester on her own.

At our closing training session, one of the trainees, Judy, handed me a thank-you note with these simple words: *Let go, let us.* She understood how wrenching it was to relinquish my hold, to share what I had created and nurtured for so long. I knew it was time, and her exquisite understanding put my mind at rest.

❀ AFFIRMATION:
There are many ways to do things right. I can learn a lot from other people.

Don't say: Look, you jerk, I've been picking your clothes up off the floor for the last twenty-five years. I quit!
                                        —The Indispensable Woman

Just because you're ready to stop being indispensable doesn't mean everybody else is primed to let you off the hook. They have a lot invested. And it takes time to renegotiate responsibilities and develop new expectations.

When we've been doing too much for too long, resentment builds up and finally boils over. Temper the temptation to dump. Being rude provides momentary relief but doesn't get us what we want. Instead of bludgeoning, ask for only one thing at a time. And say please.

❖ AFFIRMATION:
I have had a part in creating these patterns. I can undo them little by little.

They intoxicate themselves with work, so they won't see how they really are.

—*Aldous Huxley*

Men have often earned the label "workaholic," yet more and more women use work as a drug.

Work is seductive; we use it to bolster our security and self-esteem. It's easy to *become* our work, to let it define us, absorb our best energy, and drown our needs in its ceaseless demands.

When work becomes our drug of choice (there's an endless supply, so be careful!) we withdraw from the other, equally important parts of life: friendship, family, love, and play.

❀ AFFIRMATION:
My life isn't working if all I do is work.

How come I can't have Donna Reed for my mother?
                                              —Zoe Stern

My nine-year-old daughter, Zoe, is infatuated with Donna Reed. She wants a mommy who wears a housedress, scrubs the kitchen floor, and greets her children with fresh-baked cookies after school.

Donna Reed and I have about as much in common as Miss America and Madonna. I wear leggings and minidresses and gratefully pay someone else to clean my house. Slice and Bake is as good as it gets.

We can beat ourselves up for not fulfilling our children's fantasies. Or we can forgive ourselves. Besides, I'm sure if she had Donna Reed, she'd want me.

✿ AFFIRMATION:
I appreciate the freedom to choose how I want to live my life.

There are only twenty-four hours in a day, but the Indispensable Woman tries to squeeze in more. Like the airlines, she's always overbooked.

—The Indispensable Woman

Here are those twenty-four hours you've been dreaming of. Leap Year! The "bonus day" that comes once every four years, just often enough for us to appreciate it!

February 29 is a little like Daylight Savings Time; we roll the clock back an hour and are infinitely grateful for that one extra hour of sleep. Even though we know it's on the calendar, we're pleasantly surprised when it happens.

Treat today like a holiday. Use it for catch-up. Or spend it doing something special for yourself, maybe something you'll remember for the next three years.

❇ AFFIRMATION:
I will leap at the opportunity to make this a memorable day.

God only had two hands, so he invented mothers.
                                    —*Common saying*

What could be more important than being a mother? I can think of nothing that asks so much of us; we are called upon to find in ourselves infinite love, tolerance, and ingenuity, and not just when we feel like it.

Motherhood is the only job description with no holidays. No day off. The demands are relentless, the sacrifice far beyond what we bargained for.

Yet nobody praises mothers. Children are small, and so is the value attached to raising them. Motherhood takes more than two hands; the wisdom, patience, and love we give must never be taken for granted.

✿ AFFIRMATION:
Being a mother is a big job. It deserves big rewards.

There's no rest for the wicked.

—Common saying

My mother always said this. I've never really understood what it means, but the ominous tone makes me
nervous.

Either, we're wicked so we don't deserve to rest.
Or, if we keep working, we'll exorcise our demons.

Both interpretations assume the worst. Their roots
lie in the concept of "original sin"—we have to pay
continually to compensate for our innate corruption.

But the premise is wrong. We are innately *good*.

✤ AFFIRMATION:
There is real peace for those who are good.

It all boils down to self-hatred. That's the source of all problems on the planet, actually.

—Oprah Winfrey

When it comes to problems, this popular talk-show host should know: she's heard them all!

Hating ourselves poisons our capacity for healthy relationships. Addiction, abuse, and all forms of dysfunction stem from self-hatred, mostly learned in our family of origin.

That's why indispensability is a vicious cycle. Our disdain for ourselves drives us to overdo. We inevitably fail, which reinforces negative feelings, and the cycle begins again.

Stop! As grown women, we can break the pattern, begin to love ourselves, and create scenarios for success.

🏵 AFFIRMATION:
As we learn to love ourselves, our lives become more manageable.

Settle for nothing less than the object of your desire.
                                    —*Alma Luz Villanueva*

We must aim high, with all our passion, for what we want in life. Happiness is our birthright.

Instead, we settle by stretching ourselves too thin. Nothing gets quality attention. In our fragmented state, we lose sight of our deepest desires.

How do we know what would make us happy? By turning down the volume so we can hear our heart speak.

❉ AFFIRMATION:
I refuse to settle.

He doesn't care whether there are dirty dishes in the sink, but I do! He doesn't care whether the laundry is folded, but I do, so it ends up on my list!

—The Indispensable Woman

Meanwhile, *our* list gets longer and longer.

A 1990 study by Berkeley sociologist Arlie Hochchild reveals that women, on average, put in a full month's more work per year than men.

From coast to coast I've heard this confirmed: women are overwhelmed with way more than their share of work because they do too much, whereas men don't do nearly enough.

Shared partnership is the only way to balance the equation. We can expect a little less of ourselves and a little more of him without compromising our standards.

AFFIRMATION:

My list is long enough.

I want to be five-years-old again for an hour.
I want to laugh a lot and cry a lot.
I want to be picked up and rocked to sleep in someone's
*   arms,*
and carried up to bed just one more time.

—Robert Fulghum

Me too.

We think we're all grown up and that being grown up means we're all done with needing to be taken care of.

Not so. The more we let ourselves be held and rocked and cared about, the more able we are to go out in the world and conduct our grown-up lives.

In the best of all possible worlds, childhood would be a sanctuary, a wellspring of love and nurturing.

Adulthood can be, too. We can nurture ourselves now, with hugs, long baths, a soothing massage; anything that makes us feel safe and warm and carried up to bed just one more time.

✿ AFFIRMATION:
Letting myself be little makes me a bigger person.

Do not be afraid.

—*Jesus*

A few years ago I was complaining to a friend, Chris, about how anxious I felt. He said, "Do you realize that 99 percent of the time you're motivated by fear?"

I was taken aback. The next day I stopped and noticed every time I felt afraid. Twenty, thirty, sixty times that day I found myself tense and frightened, mostly about not being able to handle all my responsibilities—my marriage, my kids, my career, my friendships, the list went on and on. Each time the fear came, I paused, took a deep breath, and repeated to myself:

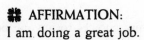 **AFFIRMATION:**
I am doing a great job.

Praise our choices, sisters, for each doorway open to us was taken by squads of fighting women who paid years of trouble and struggle, who paid their wombs, their sleep, their lives that we might walk through these gates upright.

—Marge Piercy

Today—International Women's Day—we celebrate the fact that we have choices, a direct result of feminism's fight for equal rights. Every gain, every open door has multiplied our opportunities to maneuver and lay claim to the corridors of power.

We must never forget the women who came before. But their battles, and the resulting rainbow of increased opportunities, don't obligate us to follow any certain path.

As we enter the twenty-first century we begin to heal the split between women working inside and outside the home. There is *no* single right choice. Each woman's life has worth. That is the lesson and the legacy of the women's movement.

AFFIRMATION:

I don't have to defend my choices to anyone but myself.

Keep breathing.

—*Sophie Tucker*

What good advice for Indispensable Women!

Breathing is basic; it keeps us alive. Yet we run until we're gasping for air, suffocating in order to get everything done.

Short, shallow breathing is a sign that we're being crushed under the weight of our lives.

Breathe slowly. Notice how gently this process occurs. Breathe again. Again. And again.

❀ AFFIRMATION:
I know how to breathe.

"Just how do you do it, Pooh?"
"Do what?" asked Pooh.
"Become so effortless."
"I don't do much of anything," he said.
"But how do all those things of yours get done?"
"They just sort of happen."

—*Benjamin Hoff*

Trying makes us nervous; we get all wound up over whether we're going fast enough and getting enough done.

Creativity abounds when we're relaxed. We become a channel for energy to flow freely and effortlessly. It's like dreaming. What a pleasure to wake up refreshed and discover how much we've accomplished!

✽ AFFIRMATION:
There's nothing to do.

Sometime in my life I wanted to stand at a window with a child and show him the lightning bugs and have him say, "Mommy, it's magic!"

—Anna Quindlen

The first time I wrote out this quotation, I mistakenly replaced the phrase "have him say" with the words, "have *me* say." There are no accidents.

We all want to recapture the wonder of childhood. To see the lightning bugs through the eyes of children returns us to a time of innocence and awe. A time when everything was new; when summer seemed an eternity and dusk fell like a soft blanket shimmering with lightning bugs and stars.

When did we replace wonder with work? When did we stop being amazed?

❁ AFFIRMATION:
I don't need a child to be a child.

If you want something done right, do it yourself.
                                        —*Common saying*

And so we do. And do. And do.

We make ourselves indispensable because we can't stand the idea of anyone mucking up our creation.

I've been living this way for decades. In grade school I hated group projects. I'd tell the other kids, "Go away and I'll do the whole thing. You can put your name on it just as long as you don't mess up my work."

We struggle to give up sole ownership and share the responsibility. When we don't, we end up lonely and exhausted. When we do, we trade perfection for partnership.

�֍ AFFIRMATION:
I can let other people have input without losing my ownership.

The great curiosity is like that. It is not a matter of volition. It is stark inner compulsion, dire necessity. And he against whom it moves has no more choice than a leaf driven in a gale.

—Milton Steinberg

This quote from *As a Driven Leaf* seemed like the perfect one for today, my birthday.

As a recovering Indispensable Woman, I am learning the difference between compulsively pushing myself to achieve and holding fast to my dream.

Stopping the compulsion to be indispensable is not about giving up everything. It is about no longer squandering our energy and instead focusing on our most sacred goals.

It is for each of us to discover why we are here on earth.

❈ AFFIRMATION:
I commit myself to relentlessly pursuing my dream.

Jobs for Bored Restless Young Housewives
                    —*Cover story*, Cosmopolitan, *1969*

That should be my *worst* problem!

To the degree popular magazines reflect reality, this is a telling statement of an era passed. I can count on one hand the bored, restless young housewives I have run across in the last ten years. Most women would give anything for the luxury of a good night's sleep and a way to stop feeling tormented over trying to meet work deadlines while keeping track of the school lunch menu while remembering to call their mother-in-law while keeping up friendships.

Don't *ever* think you're not doing enough. Just keeping track of everything is a full-time job in itself.

❀ AFFIRMATION:
I do more than enough.

Childhood and old age are the stages of life without any conscious problems, which is why I have not taken them into consideration here.

—Carl Gustav Jung

Childhood and old age are the bookends between which our lives are held. As children, our job is to learn; in old age we transform knowledge into wisdom.

In between, we make our mark. The pressure to decide who we are—to perform, produce, and fulfill our potential—wracks us with self-doubt.

If we can recover the playfulness of childhood and trust in safely reaching our final destination, we can move through our thirties, forties, fifties, and sixties with security and serenity.

❋ AFFIRMATION:
What's the rush?

Being humble doesn't mean one has to be a mat. What it means is, I will make myself so fine that I will be of use to you, make myself useful, do what I can do, and be an instrument of God.

—*Maya Angelou*

Humility has nothing to do with martyrdom. Humility means we see our greatness against the backdrop of the universe. Martyrdom places us in the center of the universe; every move we make takes on extraordinary importance.

Humility frees us to be of service. We give willingly, without fear of being sapped, without expectation of rewards. The resentment born of martyrdom is replaced by gratitude for having the opportunity to make a contribution. We are elevated by it.

❁ AFFIRMATION:

My humility is in perfect proportion to my self-love.

Secret: You push love out of your life by not telling your-self and others the truth about who you are and what you need.

— *Barbara De Angelis*

We want so much for other people to love us. Why else would we make ourselves indispensable?

Ironically, the more indispensable we are, the less lovable we become. We enclose ourselves in armor and push people away. Their attempts at love and support can't penetrate the wall that surrounds us.

When it comes to intimate relationships, loving is a greater gift than being loved. When was the last time you let someone love you?

✿ AFFIRMATION:
I am worthy of love.

Admire the world for never ending on you—as you would admire an opponent, without taking your eyes from him, or walking away.

—*Annie Dillard*

It is a great comfort that regardless of our actions, the world remains steady and solid. The sky above, the earth beneath our feet can be counted on to be there no matter how well we do or how badly we screw up.

The world is a constant. It is our relationships that are always in flux. We can be attentive and engage fully, or we can relinquish our hold on life, using indispensability as a way to check out.

 **AFFIRMATION:**
I am of this world. I choose to be in it.

> *#20. Color-code the kids' clothes, put in zip-lock bags, and label.*
>
> —The Indispensable Woman

Okay, I admit it. Before leaving on business trips, I organize the childrens' clothing into color-coordinated outfits, two for each day.

God forbid they should go somewhere and have someone say: "Look, there're Ellen Sue's disheveled orphans with mismatched clothes."

Not long ago Zoe accused me of being the "Clothes Police." We both laughed and then made a mother/daughter contract befitting her newfound nine-year-old maturity. She can wear what she wants to school as long as it doesn't have holes in it; for Sunday school and other dress-up occasions, I get to put my two cents in.

I'm trying to see her as a separate person, not as a reflection of myself.

✖ AFFIRMATION:
They'll never learn if I keep doing it for them.

Eat when you're hungry. Drink when you're thirsty. Sleep when you're tired.

—*Buddhist saying*

Indispensable Women are seriously estranged from themselves. Instead of responding respectfully to our internal clock, we eat on the run, drink when parched, fall into bed when we've completely run out of steam.

We pay dearly for being out of touch; our health suffers, our spirituality erodes for lack of connection to the natural rhythm of our lives.

We are not machines. We are human beings whose bodies need to be fed, watered, and given respite in order to survive.

❁ AFFIRMATION:
Taking care of my most basic needs is the foundation of my well-being.

> *I did not lose myself all at once. I rubbed out my face over the years, washing away my pain, the same way carvings on stone are worn down by water.*
>
> —Amy Tan

We desperately seek to recover our lost self by being indispensable. We want to be someone important, someone with lots to do, someone without whom other people would be lost.

The problem is, the shut-down parts of ourselves can only be healed through grieving and coming to terms. They cannot be restored by covering scars with a mask, however beautiful and elaborate.

Look in the mirror. Look deeply into your eyes. You will see who you were then and who you are now.

❈ AFFIRMATION:
I had to hide. Now it is safe to wear my own face.

*I hate housework! You make the beds, you do the dishes—
and six months later you have to start all over again.*
                                                    —Joan Rivers

Don't you love it! It would be nice to have a sense of
humor about the rumpled sheets, the dishes piled
high in the sink that make you feel like creeping back
under the covers the next morning.

The fact is, whatever sits will still be there tomorrow. We can obsess about it and feel bad about
ourselves for what we haven't finished, or we can con-
gratulate ourselves for all we've done.

❀ AFFIRMATION:
I am an adult. I can do things on my own schedule.

A touch is enough to let us know we're not alone in the universe, even in sleep.

—Adrienne Rich

I was at a dinner party last night with some close friends. The conversation turned to sex, and three different women said it had been months since they'd made love. They'd been too tired, too busy, too distracted to bother.

Touch—whether an affectionate hug or an unforgettably hot encounter—is one of the great casualties of indispensability. We can't shift gears enough to relax and get in the mood. When we're in overdrive, it's hard to remember how good sex can make us feel.

Even if it requires a leap of faith, *make* making love a priority.

❀ AFFIRMATION:
Making love is not another job. It feels good and it's good for me.

I decided to stop doing my two teen-aged sons' laundry. I bought each of them a hamper and watched it pile up for three weeks. Then one morning I overheard them in the bathroom. The first said, "Do you have any clean underwear?" "No," said the second. "Okay," replied the first, "let's switch."

— *I.W. workshop participant*

A woman in a workshop in Shreveport, Louisiana, told this story. Everyone howled.

If we do everything ourselves, we get to do it *our* way. But when we give some of the responsibility back to its rightful owners, we have to move out of their way.

Gradually we get used to other people's ways of doing things. We may never be thrilled by their style or standards, but it sure frees us to concentrate on our own lives.

❋ AFFIRMATION:
My time is valuable. I won't waste it doing things that other people are fully capable of doing for themselves.

Just to be is a blessing.
Just to live is holy.

—*Abraham Heschel*

Have you ever been present at the birth of a baby? In the instant of birth, everyone there—mother, father, friends, and medical staff—is awestruck at the sacred quality of the experience.

We stare at the brand-new baby, marveling at its perfection, saying prayers of thanksgiving for its miraculous arrival. No one asks the newborn baby: What do *you* do for a living?

Being born is all anyone could ask for, and then some.

❈ AFFIRMATION:
My life is as holy as the day I was born.

> *Ultimately, scare tactics aren't enough. We need to have a positive vision.*
>
> —The Indispensable Woman

In my workshops I ask women to imagine what it would be like to stop making themselves indispensable. "Serene," says one woman. "Spontaneous," says another. "Divorced," says a third, half jokingly.

We have so much to gain by giving up our indispensability—health, vitality, time for ourselves. We get off the treadmill and find a calmer, more natural pace.

We also lose some things. Attention. The illusion of control. Change—even positive change—always meets with resistance. It's easy to fall back into old patterns if we aren't moving toward a compelling goal.

❊ AFFIRMATION:
I have so much to look forward to.

I think it pisses God off if you walk by the color purple in a field somewhere and don't notice it.

— *Alice Walker*

I live next door to Michael, who spends hours planting flowers in his front yard.

Meanwhile, I sit at my computer, struggling to plant seeds of my own, sometimes working for hours and hours without walking outside to take in the fresh spring leaves making their appearance on the oak tree between our houses.

The world overflows with beauty, much of which we miss when we make ourselves indispensable. Nature waits patiently for us to notice the purples, greens, and golds.

❄ AFFIRMATION:
I am entitled to experience joy.

It is easier to live through someone else than to become complete yourself.

—Betty Friedan

It's part of why we have children. Or rescue stray puppies. Or keep draining ourselves doing all the "emotional work" in our marriage, which keeps our mate conveniently off the hook.

Being a whole person is hard work. It's much easier to focus on fixing other people than to grapple with our own intractable egos.

Of course, when we overly invest in other people or dogs or plants or anything outside ourselves, we set ourselves up. They grow up or die or simply get tired of being the object of our distraction.

The best insurance against emptiness is learning to live fully within ourselves.

❋ AFFIRMATION:
I am only responsible for living one life—mine.

> *You depend on God, not God on you.*
> —*Bahya Ibn Pakudah*

What a relief! It takes an enormous burden off our shoulders to get *that* straight!

As children, our security comes from trusting that the grown-ups have their act together. Sometimes they do, sometimes they don't. As adults, if we can surrender some part of our burden to a higher power, we move more lightly through life.

Many people resist Step Three of the Twelve Steps: "We made a decision to turn our will and our lives" over to a power greater than ourselves—interpreting it as copping out, ducking responsibility, opting for mindless dependency.

Nothing could be further from the truth. True surrender requires great courage and strength of character.

✽ AFFIRMATION:
I don't have to do it all alone.

"Acting out," said Rosalie bitterly, flicking ash from her small black cheroot, "is what the rest of us call living."
—Lynne Sharon Schwartz, Disturbances in the Field

We are the self-help generation; we've labeled every conceivable behavior, hoping to "work on ourselves" until we get it right.

Maybe we're working too hard. We analyze every nuance, pushing ourselves in our personal growth as if every week were "finals week." We feel bad when we "act out" or "slip" or fall into the same old trap for the hundredth time.

Self-examination is the road to enlightenment. But so are laughter . . . and swimming . . . and sleep.

AFFIRMATION:
I don't have to work so hard.

Hi.
How am I?

—*Rokelle Lerner*

Author and speaker Roxy Lerner was quoted as rec-
ommending these words for silk screening on the
front of T-shirts for codependents. At a convention of
Indispensable Women, they'd sell like hotcakes.

We look to others to tell whether we're doing an
okay job. If they say yes—with a smile, a raise, a
dinner invitation—we feel good about ourselves. But
that good feeling is quickly destroyed by any intima-
tion that we've let someone down.

As long as we give away our power, we are on
shaky ground. We are on solid ground when we can
proudly wear a T-shirt that says:

❀ **AFFIRMATION:**
Hi. I'm fine.

Grass doesn't grow on a busy street.

—*Anonymous*

My friend Chloe, age six, is the spitting image of Shirley Temple, golden curls and all. But until turning four, she was nearly bald, which prompted her Grandma Marilyn to make the above comment.

We can't always see visible or immediate results from our efforts. Real growth takes time; ever so slowly the ground thaws and the blades of grass poke through. Spring surprises us again!

Knowing how to wait—with trust and confidence in the unseen—is a great challenge for Indispensable Women who want everything *right now*! It is a daily discipline.

❋ AFFIRMATION:
None of my effort is wasted.

Wisdom is learning what to overlook.

—William James

Picky, picky, picky! As Vice President for Quality Control, we see to it that everything is up to code. Nothing escapes our eagle eye. No mistakes are forgiven.

Learning what to overlook—or when to look the other way—is an acquired skill. It takes discipline and concentration to discriminate between what to focus our energies on and what to ignore.

Letting the little things go doesn't mean we're falling down on the job. We're simply saving our expertise for when it's really needed.

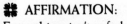 AFFIRMATION:
Everything isn't a federal case.

When the going gets tough, the tough go shopping.
                              —*Bumper sticker*

Indispensable Women are vulnerable to addiction; we
refuel with shopping, sugar, pills—anything to pump
ourselves up and fill the emptiness inside.

When we operate at a deficit, we need constant
rewards. It's a vicious cycle. We race around, exhaust
ourselves, down another cup of coffee and another
chocolate doughnut to keep going until we crash
again and the cycle repeats itself.

Back when I smoked three packs a day, cigarettes
were my reward. Now, when I reach a goal, I give
myself a break simply to sit and appreciate what I've
accomplished.

❀ AFFIRMATION:
When the going gets tough, I can take a break.

When I'm meeting with a family to prepare a eulogy, nobody ever says of the deceased: "I wish she'd spent more time working."

—Rabbi Joseph Black

Have you ever fantasized about listening to your own eulogy? What would others say about you? What words would they choose to sum up your life?

How we live today is what will be remembered. In the end, no one will care how many raises we got or whether we met the impossible deadline.

What will count is the kind of person we were. Did we make time for loved ones in our lives? Were we thoughtful? Caring? Compassionate?

❉ AFFIRMATION:
Today I will live as if there were no tomorrow.

If I wasn't wearing it, I'd be washing it.
                    —*Saying on front of an I.W. T-shirt*

A friend, Bonnie, suggested this wonderful slogan, which still makes me laugh.

It's never okay for Indispensable Women just to sit still. We fold the laundry while we watch TV, jot shopping lists while we're making business calls . . .

What if we didn't do *anything* for ten minutes? An hour? A day? What would we discover about ourselves?

✿ AFFIRMATION:
Today I will experiment with being perfectly still for ten minutes just to see how it feels.

Women, in whom life lingers and dwells more immediately, more fruitfully, and more confidently, must surely have become riper and more human in their depths than light, easygoing man. . . .

— *Rainer Maria Rilke*

We are exquisite human beings! Our inherent connection to birth and death, to the gentle turnings of the moon and the tides, makes us intensely aware of life's sanctity.

In our efforts to achieve, we must resist imitating masculine models. It may still be a man's world, but we are changing it with our softness and humanity.

❉ AFFIRMATION:
I'd rather be a woman.

Recovery is a process, not an event.

—*Anne Wilson Schaef*

We take on recovery as if it were a marathon. Get ready . . . Get set . . . Go!

Indispensable Women run the risk of being over-achievers even in our recovery. We have to get better immediately!

Recovery is a slow journey of small, carefully navigated steps: the one time we say, "No, I can't drive the carpool today"; the one time we ask a friend to be there, just because we need a shoulder to cry on.

Every step is a step in the right direction.

❋ AFFIRMATION:
I will be easy on myself.

Ask your child what he wants for dinner only if he's buying.

—Fran Lebowitz

Sometimes I feel like a short-order cook. One wants artichokes, the other wants macaroni and cheese.

Mothers who work outside the home tend to feel especially guilty when our children express disappointment. We're already indicted by our failure to be 24-hour-a-day moms; we pay our debt to society by being at their beck and call.

Setting firm boundaries with our children—saying how far we will go and sticking to it—makes them feel secure. And security makes them feel loved.

❀ AFFIRMATION:
My children will still love me if I say no.

They say you should not suffer through the past. You should be able to wear it like a loose garment, take it off and let it drop.

—Eva Jessye

We torment ourselves with past mistakes, agonizing over what we could have done differently.

It's time to stop dragging ourselves down, wearing our failures like a heavy winter coat. We couldn't have done anything differently, or we would have! We were who we were then. We are who we are now.

❉ **AFFIRMATION:**
I'm done paying for my mistakes.

You can never be too thin or too rich.
                    —*The Duchess of Windsor*

Sometimes attributed to Gloria Guiness or Babe Paley, this was a famous nugget of wisdom during my growing-up years. Although I knew the advice was half-joking, that didn't keep me from dieting feverishly.

We *can* be too thin, as those of us who've struggled with eating disorders know too well. Driving ourselves until we become anorexic or workaholic is dangerous. Every bite of food fills us with anxiety; work becomes strictly a means to an end instead of a source of satisfaction.

In moderation, eating can be a pleasure! And work a source of satisfaction in itself.

✿ **AFFIRMATION:**
I will satisfy myself.

I can have a fabulous day at the office, but if I come home and the kitchen floor is sticky, I feel like a failure.
                                        —The Indispensable Woman

This is what I call a "nontransferrable credit"—we do well in one area of our lives but the satisfaction doesn't spill over into the next.

We hold ourselves to such high standards that we aren't ever satisfied. We're on to the next task instead of taking a well-deserved minute to stop and *kvell* (Yiddish for taking pleasure and pride).

Make a conscious effort to give yourself credit where credit is due.

✽ AFFIRMATION:
I will pay as much attention to my accomplishments as my failures.

Time is the relationship between events.
                              —*Yakima Indian Nation*

For Indispensable Women, time is the most precious commodity. There's never enough of it; worrying about it makes us anxious and less efficient.

We relate to time as if it were a stern taskmaster standing over our shoulder. Faster. Faster. Time saved is money in the bank.

In fact, time has no concrete value. It cannot be saved or squandered, it simply is.

❈ AFFIRMATION:
I have plenty of time.

If only God would give me some clear sign! Like making a large deposit in my name at a Swiss bank.

—*Woody Allen*

How do we know whether we're doing what we're supposed to do with our lives?

Maybe that's why Indispensable Women keep doing so much; we want all our bases covered.

Sheer exhaustion, contrary to popular opinion, doesn't prove anything other than the fact that we've used ourselves up. Inner peace is the only sure sign that we're investing our energies in the right direction.

❀ AFFIRMATION:
I am on the right track.

> *"You won't give anybody a chance,"* said Laurie, a little
> color rising in his cheeks. *"When anybody does see the soft*
> *side of you, you throw cold water on him."*
> *"I don't like that sort of thing. I'm too busy to be worried*
> *with nonsense, so let's change the subject,"* said Jo crossly.
> —Louisa May Alcott, Little Women

Little Women was my favorite book when I was growing
up. I liked it because Meg, Jo, Beth, and Amy were so
different, one from the other: responsible Meg, independent Jo, dear, sweet Beth, and flirtatious Amy,
whose charm and conceit inevitably got her into trouble.

Of them all, I worried most about Jo. True to her
era, she was forced to make a choice, suppressing her
softness to pursue writing, her real passion.

Too many Indispensable Women do the same. We
may be married, we may be involved in an intimate
relationship, but our work distances us from our lovers; we can't be soft and successful at the same time.

I hope my daughter reads *Little Women*, knowing
there is a way to integrate all sides of ourselves.

❇ **AFFIRMATION:**
I accept every part of myself.

There's no place like home.
                    —Dorothy, The Wizard of Oz

Home can be a sanctuary to Indispensable Women, always on the run. Yet too often we use home as a way station for grabbing our mail and messages and changing clothes before racing to our next appointment.

When we're out and about, we tend to be "on"; our facade is always in place while we conduct our worldly business, be it running a meeting or driving our children to piano lessons.

At home we can let down. Recharge. Recover the strength it takes to make our mark in the world.

✿ **AFFIRMATION:**
At home I can be myself.

People ask you for criticism, but they only want praise.
—*W. Somerset Maugham*

Indispensable Women are expert advisors! When
someone asks our opinion, we think they want our
carefully considered analysis. Just listening isn't
enough; we have to add insight, or what good are we?

We confuse support and advice. We mistakenly
take people at face value when they ask, "What do
you think?" Music to our ears!

More often than not, our brilliant perceptions are
met with annoyance or anger. Be careful. The next
time someone turns to you, really listen to what
they're asking. Is your critique welcome? Or do they
only want their point of view reinforced?

❇ AFFIRMATION:
Is my advice coming from a loving place or is it a
way to feel important?

> *If you want to live in this world, equip yourself with a*
> *heart that can endure suffering.*
>
> —*Midrash: Leviticus Rabbah*

It is true that suffering is a crucible. That it builds character.

Suffering makes us sensitive and compassionate—admirable qualities to be sure. But there can be too much of a good thing. For Indispensable Women, suffering is a baseline; we live with heavy hearts, painfully aware of other people's burdens as well as our own.

To live in this world we also need hearts filled with joy. Happiness builds character too.

❋ **AFFIRMATION:**
My heart needn't be heavy to be full.

#12. Tape a picture of myself inside Evan's lunchbox.
                    —The Indispensable Woman

In retrospect, we see how funny our indispensability is. The time we spent four hours cleaning the bathtub only to discover we'd scraped the caulking off. The time we had the babysitter wake the sleeping children so we could say good night.

When we're in the thick of it, nothing's funny. We take ourselves *very* seriously. If we can lighten up a bit, most things fall into much better perspective.

❄ **AFFIRMATION:**
Few things are as serious as they seem.

A patronizing disposition always has its meaner side.
— George Eliot

Everyone resents being patronized. Even if we know we're right, we need to curb our tendency to treat other people as if they were children.

Our efforts to "educate" belie feelings of disdain. And insecurity. We put other people down in order to stay up. We do it subtly through tone of voice, body language, or sentence construction ("Don't you think that's a weird way of looking at things?"), or blatantly ("That's the weirdest thing I've ever heard!").

Indispensability rests on the firm belief in our inherent superiority. The more we can instruct other people, the more we can verify our own worth.

Wouldn't it be nice to go on sabbatical? To let someone else be professor for a change?

❀ AFFIRMATION:
I am secure enough to be a student.

Just say no.

—*Nancy Reagan*

Easier said than done, as we've seen with this dubious campaign in the country's ongoing War on Drugs.

Recovery from addiction is far more complex than simply saying no. Whatever our drug of choice—be it alcohol, gambling, or indispensability—recovery is a daily process.

Just saying no suggests that willpower is all it takes. But abstinence goes much further; it requires facing down the demons demanding attention in the form of a fix.

We mustn't be sanguine about recovery. It's the bravest step we can take. Ultimately, it has little to do with saying no, and lots to do with saying yes—yes to health, yes to sanity, yes to serenity.

❧ AFFIRMATION:
Yes.

We are determined to be starved before we are hungry.
—Henry David Thoreau

When I was recovering from a serious depression, a friend, Rhoda, called to ask how I was doing. "Much better!" I told her. "Now I'll be able to think more clearly and get more done!"

"Wait a minute," she said. "What about getting better so you can have a better life?"

I was taken aback. I was so used to focusing on work, it hadn't even occurred to me that enhanced quality of life could be a goal!

We're accustomed to the stress and strain caused by our indispensability. It becomes routine. Until we hit bottom—getting sick, divorced, or making a costly mistake on the job—we never notice how starved we are for nourishment and rest.

We don't need to collapse in order to get well. A little pampering is preventive medicine.

❊ AFFIRMATION:
I will feel my hunger and feed myself.

If you would shut your door against the children for an hour a day and say: "Mother is working on her five-act tragedy in blank verse!" you would be surprised how they would respect you. They would probably all become playwrights.

—Brenda Euland

Mothers with careers are terrific role models. In pursuing our ambitions, we make it possible for our children to see the myriad possibilities.

The trade-off is being less available to our children. I still struggle to reconcile my expectations (here comes Donna Reed again!) with the realities of a demanding, time-consuming career.

It's a gift to our children to see moms as people in their own right, successful in the world. It's a gift to ourselves—and an obligation—to follow our dreams.

❀ AFFIRMATION:
I am a person first.

*The world is imprisoned by its own activity, except when
actions are performed as worship of God.*

—Bhagavad Gita

Indispensability is a prison of our own making.
"There's nothing I can do about how much I have to
do!" we say, locked behind the prison bars of our own
self-victimization.

Choice is the key to freedom. When we choose to
do something, even if doing it is difficult or time-
consuming, we feel good. We feel powerful and free
because no one is forcing us against our will.

It is our responsibility to unlock the prison doors
by making positive choices, choices that express our
genuine commitment and love.

❀ AFFIRMATION:
I am not a victim. I can choose to say yes or no.

Expect a miracle.

—*Popular bumper sticker*

I've always loved this saying. When I'm driving in the car and see it, I feel like waving the driver over so I can find out whether any miracle has happened to that person today.

What are miracles? Moments of serendipity—running into someone we haven't seen for twenty years and becoming business partners; meeting the love of our life in the airport while waiting for a flight that's been postponed because of engine trouble. Miracles occur each and every day. The real challenge is in recognizing and receiving them.

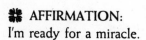 **AFFIRMATION:**
I'm ready for a miracle.

If the kids are still alive when my husband comes home, I've done my job.

—Roseanne Arnold

There are days like that! Days when our patience is shot, when we're just plain out of energy and the thought of reading one more story or starting one more art project makes us wish we'd run off to a nunnery.

Those are the days when we need to cut ourselves some slack. Hire a baby-sitter. Rent a video. Let them eat peanut butter out of the jar while you take a bath and a break.

Forget "Mother of the Year." Some days, just getting through is fine.

❈ AFFIRMATION:
I'm doing a great job.

I'm the only one who can do it.

—The Indispensable Woman

Are you *really* the only one who can do it? Could someone else do part of it? What if you were sick and couldn't do it at all?

We need to examine our assumptions rigorously. What we believe dictates how we act. If we assume that we're the only one who can do it, we'll do it all. If we adjust our assumptions—"I can do all of it or I can do part of it"—we expand our choices. And get much-needed help.

❀ AFFIRMATION:
I will pay attention to the voices inside my head.

The hardest work of all is to do nothing.

—*Jewish saying*

We experience a void when we stop making ourselves indispensable. The void is foreign and scary; our first impulse is to fall back into habitual behavior, filling it with compulsive activity. Anything to avoid the looming emptiness inside.

To be able to be alone with ourselves, simply being, is the best test of our recovery from indispensability. What seems threatening is actually a gift. The void is an opening, an opportunity to feel our yearning for a more peaceful, balanced life.

❈ AFFIRMATION:
Emptiness is a state of readiness.

She was tired. It was as simple as that. This life she loved so much had been lived, all along, with the greatest effort.
—Ann Beattie

We can't possibly appreciate our lives when we can barely keep our eyes open.

Indispensable Women are TIRED. We wear ourselves out doing too much and then wonder why we're not having any fun.

There is no substitute for rest. Without it, what's pleasurable becomes drudgery and we turn into drudges. Rest, even a little, replenishes our energy and makes us a pleasure to be around.

❧ AFFIRMATION:
Resting is not a last resort. It is a necessary part of life.

Preparing for the worst is an activity I have taken up since I turned thirty-five, and the worst actually began to happen.
—*Delia Ephron*

Expecting the worst—and taking pains to prepare for it—keeps us rooted in our indispensability. Just think how much work there is to do to head off the end of the world!

A crisis mentality adds drama to our lives. We rationalize our frenetic level of activity by thinking of ourselves as firefighters, poised to climb up the ladder, hearts pounding, ready to put out the fire.

Preparing for the worst also preempts disappointment. It is a way of exercising control to combat feelings of powerlessness. The reward: We get to keep *doing* something. The cost: We *have* to keep doing something.

❉ AFFIRMATION:
What if the worst never comes?

Women hold up half the sky.

—*Buddhist saying*

The operative word is *half.*

Holding up the sky—doing all the incredible things women do—is way beyond what any human being should ask of herself.

Yet we ask more. We stand on our tiptoes, straining to balance the horizon on our fingertips, not to mention the moon, the sun, and the stars.

It's time to let men hold up their half of the sky. Men can change diapers, wash dishes, hire baby-sitters, and make plans for Saturday night. Men can do anything if we get out of their way and let them.

❀ **AFFIRMATION:**
I'm holding more than my own. It's time to hand some of it over.

If you think you can, you can. If you think you can't, you can't.

—Henry Ford

Indispensable Women waste enormous amounts of energy worrying about whether we can do it well enough, instead of just getting out there and getting it done.

Fear of failure short-circuits success. The only way to know what we're capable of is to try.

Self-doubt — stemming from perfectionism — plagues and prevents us from reaching our goals.

We transcend self-doubt by cultivating confidence. Real confidence—based on self-love, not bravado—is a lifelong pursuit in which we say to ourselves:

✿ AFFIRMATION:
I can do it.

Women sometimes seem to share a quiet, unalterable dogma of persecution. . . .

—Zelda Fitzgerald

Being a martyr doesn't heal the hurt.

We have all been hurt. Each of us has experienced pain or persecution sometime in our lives. But making ourselves indispensable to prove how hard we've had it only makes it worse.

We cannot restore power and security lost in childhood. That time is gone. Forever. We *can* take charge of our lives now. The present holds the best healing: to choose our own direction; to go forward as a free agent.

❦ AFFIRMATION:
I am nobody's victim.

#6. Leave guilt gifts for the children under their pillows.
— *I.W. seminar*

Susan, a corporate vice president who's constantly on the road, warned me against returning home from business trips laden with gifts. She said, "I started out doing that and pretty soon my kids couldn't wait for me to leave!"

We overcompensate for perceived imperfections. We let our children stay up past ten because they've had a baby-sitter two nights in a row. We indulge them with treats and sweets and other forbidden fruits in order to assuage our guilt for not being "perfect mothers."

The more we give, the less we're giving of what's really valuable: the gift of seeing one's parents as real people. Perfectly imperfect.

❈ AFFIRMATION:
I am a good enough mother.

I have a new philosophy. I'm only going to dread one day at a time.

—Charlie Brown (Charles Schulz)

This makes great sense. If we have to worry, we may as well get it into manageable bites.

Indispensable Women's chronic headaches and stiff muscles come from flooding our nervous systems with anxiety and dread. Anxiety over whether we'll be able to do it all; dread over what will happen if we don't.

Nothing will happen. If we take one day at a time —the soundest recovery advice of all—we can think straight and deal sanely with the next thing on our list.

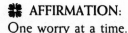 **AFFIRMATION:**
One worry at a time.

tell all your daughters
to build something better
burn kindling
not carry
keep one eye on the sky.

—Mary Mackey

It is good to strive—to know what we want and reach for it from the depths of our being.

Indispensability and striving are not the same, just as grasping and reaching are not the same. We make ourselves indispensable as if our lives depended on it; we strive, knowing our lives will be enriched for having given it our all.

✿ AFFIRMATION:
Everything is within my reach.

> *Marrying a man is like buying something you've been admiring for a long time in a shop window. You may love it when you get it home, but it doesn't always go with everything in the house.*
> —*Jean Kerr,* The Snake Has All the Lines

Indispensable Women are obsessed with making improvements. Once when I was out of town, a friend visiting from New York stayed at my apartment. When I returned, she'd rearranged the furniture.

We are especially interested in upgrading our mates. As soon as we get our hands on them, we try to remake them to suit our specifications. Their hair could be a little shorter, their conversation more colorful, and *why* can't they put the catsup bottle back where it belongs?

The better question is: Why can't *we* leave well enough alone! He doesn't have to match our color scheme—the real art is to appreciate the contrasts.

❦ AFFIRMATION:
Our differences are complementary.

> *"Where did you go to, if I may ask?"* said Thorin to Gandalf as they rode along.
> *"To look ahead,"* said he.
> *"And what brought you back in the nick of time?"*
> *"Looking behind,"* said he.
>
> —J.R.R. Tolkien

We're usually one step ahead of ourselves. We head-trip about the future, obsessing about what hasn't even happened yet.

It's important to look behind us from time to time, to take stock and gain wisdom from our experience.

Looking ahead helps us know where we're going; looking back helps us remember why we headed there in the first place.

✿ AFFIRMATION:
I will look both ways.

Whatever women do they must do twice as well as men to be thought half as good. Luckily, this is not difficult.
—Charlotte Whitton

This may sound mean, but most women agree: The world still expects more from us than from men, without offering nearly the same rewards.

Indispensable Women counter by being three and four times as good, an exhausting, senseless pursuit based on the premise that in order to succeed, we must better men's efforts in their arenas and on their terms.

Their terms will kill us, just as they are killing them. With our native intelligence, intuition, and strength, we can and must redefine the meaning of success.

❀ AFFIRMATION:
I need not compete with men in order to succeed.

> *To laugh often and much;*
> *To win the respect of intelligent*
> *people and the affection of children,*
> *to earn the appreciation of honest critics*
> *and endure the betrayal of false friends;*
> *to appreciate beauty, to find the best in others,*
> *to leave the world a bit better whether by a*
> *healthy child, a garden patch, or a redeemed*
> *social condition; to know even one life has*
> *breathed easier because you lived.*
> *This is to have succeeded.*
>
> —*Ralph Waldo Emerson*

This quotation was sent as a tribute to my father-in-law, Lester Stern, when he died.

Emerson's qualifications for a successful life are sound standards for Indispensable Women. I find the first line particularly hopeful; that even before we go about winning anyone's respect or earning appreciation, we laugh often and much.

It's so easy to forget that life is supposed to be fun.

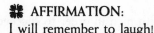 **AFFIRMATION:**
I will remember to laugh!

Do you secretly believe that no one can do it as well, as fast, as efficiently as you?

—The Indispensable Woman

" They can't!" shouts out one woman at an I.W. seminar in Chicago.

Most Indispensable Women readily admit to trusting only themselves to get the job done right. Other people may be capable of slipshod, perhaps even passable work. But excellence? Out of the question!

Arrogance is the single biggest obstacle to recovery. Until we see that other people's styles are different but equal, we're stuck doing everything ourselves.

❄ AFFIRMATION:
Once in a while I can be a team player.

> *I believed in change. I believed in metamorphosis. I believed in redemption.*
>
> —*Nora Ephron*

In her novel, *Heartburn*, quoted above, Nora Ephron's heroine explains why she kept hanging on to a bad marriage: "My marriage to him was as willful an act as I've ever committed. I married him against all the evidence."

Indispensable Woman Recovery Lesson #2: There is no changing anyone.

We knock ourselves out waiting and hoping for him to catch up and come through. Meanwhile we wear ourselves to a frazzle; we lose our sleep, our friends, and the last shreds of our self-respect because we can't let go, even when it's over.

Accepting reality—what is, *is*, what *isn't*, isn't likely to appear—frees us to get on with our lives, even if it means being alone.

❄ **AFFIRMATION:**
My life is too precious to waste trying to change another person.

There will be sex after death, we just won't be able to feel it.

—Lily Tomlin

Lots of us don't feel it now. We're living in our heads, numb from the neck down.

When I conduct I.W. seminars, I meet scores of women who've stopped having sex, stopped enjoying it, or both. They don't have time. Or they just put up with it, counting the minutes until they can go to sleep.

If we wait to make love until the laundry is folded or the kids are at camp or the millions are made, we may die missing some of the sweetest pleasure life has to offer.

If, for whatever reason, sex is too big of a leap, get a massage. Or sit in a sauna. Do something to feel how silky and sensual you are.

❀ AFFIRMATION:
I deserve to feel good.

When we can't dream any longer, we die.

—*Emma Goldman*

We get so wrapped up in other people's dreams, ours never get off the ground.

When we put our dreams on hold, we cheat ourselves and the world of our promise. Deferred dreams die. They deflate like leftover balloons from a child's birthday, slowly sinking in the corner.

We must breathe air into our own balloons. Tie them with beautiful ribbons. Admire them. Honor them. Give them flight.

✿ AFFIRMATION:
My dreams are real.

I have met brave women who are exploring the outer edge of human possibility, with no history to guide them, and with a courage to make themselves vulnerable that I find moving beyond words.

—Gloria Steinem

Indispensability is an evolutionary phase—a transition between shedding old skin and acquiring a new one.

It takes time to get comfortable. After generations of defining ourselves in relation to others—Billy's mother, David's wife, Eleanor's mother—we aren't sure who we are anymore. What's old is familiar. Must we discard the pattern and begin anew?

Times of transition require vision, tenacity, and a basket nearby in which to keep the cast-off remnants of material. Slowly but surely we find the right fit.

❄ AFFIRMATION:
I needed to make myself indispensable. Someday I won't.

There is no room for God in the man who is filled with himself.

—*Baal Shem Tov*

Humility is admitting we need help, making room for others to help and guide us, whether it's loving friends, professional counselors, or a higher power in whom we place our trust.

We are not alone and we needn't have all the answers. When we act as if we do, we convince other people there's nothing for them to give.

Need is not weakness or a sign of failure; humility is the courage to say:

❀ AFFIRMATION:
Help.

In the final analysis it is not what you do for your children but what you have taught them to do for themselves that will make them successful human beings.

—Ann Landers

Doing everything for our children, rather than teaching them to do for themselves, appeals to Indispensable Women for two reasons: we control the outcome, and we get to be our children's hero or servant—depending on how you look at it.

In the short run, doing for our children gets things done. Over the long term, we're not doing anyone a favor. We deplete ourselves, build up resentment, and prevent our children from learning valuable life skills that will serve them long after we're gone.

❊ AFFIRMATION:
I am my children's teacher, not their slave.

> *Wouldn't you get pissed off if you had to initiate every single conversation about your marriage for the past twenty years?*
>
> —The Indispensable Woman

We get sick of being the facilitators of our relationships, keeping up both ends of the conversation like a ventriloquist with a dummy on her lap.

Yet we continue to bring up issues in the face of our partner's silence. What's the deal? Is he perfectly satisfied, or doesn't he care enough about the relationship to work at it?

Processing isn't the only way to be closer. Playing, doing a project around the house, watching a favorite TV show together are ways of building intimacy without creating a scene.

�֎ AFFIRMATION:
I will let things happen naturally.

People change and forget to tell each other.
                                        —*Lillian Hellman*

Indispensable Women move rapidly, whether maneuvering through traffic or marking important passages in our lives.

When our partner's growth isn't as fast or visible as ours, we get panicky. We worry we've outdistanced him and he will vanish from our rearview mirror.

People grow at their own rate. We get there when we get there, and there's no rushing it.

What's important is to communicate. We can't expect another person to follow our twists and turns without a map. We need to share how we're changing if we want our traveling companions to keep up.

✻ AFFIRMATION:
I am responsible for telling other people what I want them to know.

Elves, we know, live on very little, and despise the coarse garments of mortals: mine sometimes wanders about without a tie and with flowing locks.

—Colette

Have you ever wondered what would happen if all your trappings of security suddenly disappeared and you had to start over?

What kind of life would you create? Would you make the same choices, or would you trade some measure of financial security for time to yourself or time with your husband, children, or friends?

Every day we must ask ourselves three questions: What do I want out of life? What trade-offs am I making? Are they worth it?

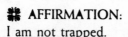 **AFFIRMATION:**
I am not trapped.

Better bend than break.

—*Swedish proverb*

Indispensable Women see things in black and white. Gray is too nebulous; shades of uncertainty threaten our rigid hold on life.

Learning to give way, to loosen our schedules, to be flexible even in the face of the completely unexpected, is essential to recovery.

Consider the palm tree. Straight and strong with its crown of leaves open to the sun. Have you ever seen one during a hurricane? The palm's hidden strength is its ability to bend yet remain standing.

❀ AFFIRMATION:
I am strong enough to bend without breaking.

There is nothing permanent except change.

—Heraclitus

Change is upsetting. I'm chronically late because I hate to leave where I am. Whenever I go somewhere, I have to force myself to get in the car. Then, by the time I arrive, I don't want to get out. I become used to wherever I am.

We yearn for permanence. For the inner security that comes from knowing we've arrived, that we've reached our destination.

But when we get there, there's somewhere else to go.

�֍ AFFIRMATION:
Every change is a new opportunity.

*If at first you don't succeed, try, try again. Then quit.
There's no use being a fool about it.*

—W. C. Fields

Indispensable Women never give up. Or give in. A
knockout decision is unthinkable; when faced with a
particularly tough challenge, we redouble our efforts
and come out fighting, with new, ingenious ways to
win.

There's a time to quit trying. When persistence
gives way to stubborn pride, it's time to get out of the
ring.

❉ AFFIRMATION:
Enough already.

Every time you do something nice for someone, follow it by doing something nice for yourself.

—The Indispensable Woman

This doesn't seem like a big deal until we actually stop and count all the favors we owe ourselves.

Everything counts. Saying "Hi. How are you?" and *really listening* to the answer. Smiling at a stranger. Offering well-thought-out advice to a friend in trouble.

We give to others as a matter of course. If we were half as generous with ourselves, we'd be saying "Thank you" all day long.

❖ AFFIRMATION:
I will treat myself as well as I treat others.

One's friends are that part of the human race with which one can be human.

—George Santayana

Our friends are our chosen family. They are our lifeline, our litmus test, the mirrors that reflect our weaknesses and strengths.

It's terribly important to surround ourselves with friends. Friends who accept us exactly as we are. Who love us even when we're mean and crabby and having trouble loving ourselves.

Dear friends are our reward for doing our recovery work.

❁ AFFIRMATION:
My friends know me and love me.

When So-so Things Happen to Average People.
                    —*Book title in "Ziggy" cartoon*

We worry whether our problems have star quality, whether they're exciting and hip enough to land us on a television talk show.

What we're really worried about is that underneath it all, we're just an ordinary person, leading an average (perish the thought!) life.

There is no such thing as an "average" person. An average amount of rainfall or length of labor, okay, but not an average person.

Each of our lives is extraordinary. Not because of the drama we create, but because our unique essence sets us apart.

❀ AFFIRMATION:
I am not like anyone else.

*In analysis, the small and lonely child that is hidden
behind his achievements wakes up and asks: "What would
have happened if I had appeared before you, bad, ugly, angry, jealous, lazy, dirty, smelly? Where would your love
have been then?"*

—Alice Miller

If you knew me, would you stick around? Indispensable Women aren't sure, so we only reveal what's ster-
ilized and safe.

We are terrified of being found out. The quirky,
messy, not-so-pretty parts of ourselves lurk behind
our shaky facade, ready to leap out like monsters in
the night.

We want desperately to be loved for who we are.
To be seen fully. In the light.

❊ AFFIRMATION:
I don't have to hide anymore.

A house does not need a wife anymore than it does a husband.

—*Charlotte Perkins Gilman*

My house doesn't have either, and it's holding up just fine.

Still, a little partnership at home goes a long way, *if* we're able to refrain from criticism.

We grab the baby out of his arms because he isn't burping her right. We ask him to do the dishes, then jump up thirty seconds later when he hasn't started and do them ourselves, fuming all the while.

Think about it: Would you want to try if it always had to be on someone else's terms?

❋ AFFIRMATION:
It doesn't have to be perfect.

Time is a dressmaker specializing in alterations.
—*Faith Baldwin*

We're impatient with ourselves, intolerant of our flaws and imperfections.

If we can see them as necessary alterations in a masterwork in progress, we can relax and enjoy who we are in the present.

With time, we refine the garment; a tuck here, a stitch there as we gradually grow into ourselves.

 **AFFIRMATION:**
I am constantly reweaving myself.

When I am an old woman I shall wear purple. . . .
—Elizabeth Lucas

We choose our words, our colors, even the food we eat, as if we were at some perpetual audition.

But "they" actually don't care. We do. In our indispensability, we constantly invent ourselves to please our audience.

As we grow older, we worry less about what other people think. We get to be outrageous or reclusive or anything else that suits us.

Maybe it's time to start now. Only fear holds us back.

AFFIRMATION:
The more I am myself, the more others will be drawn to me.

The turning point is that moment of naked acceptance of the truth. Denial falls away like scales from our eyes.
                                    —The Indispensable Woman

There comes a moment when we realize how much we are hurting ourselves. We get sick. Our marriage suffers from neglect. Friends drift away one by one, because we never give them the time of day.

Is it inevitable to hit bottom? Or can we begin the process of recovery without first getting hit over the head with serious consequences?

Why wait for a near or total breakdown? If you're overtired, overwhelmed, or undernourished, these are signs that it's time to start recovering balance in your life. Act now. Make today a positive turning point.

❄ AFFIRMATION:
I am ready to begin recovery.

A woman's place . . . is in a restaurant.

—*Greeting card*

These days a woman's place is anywhere she wants to be. The down side is that all too often, we're in six or seven places at once.

In the high-pressure nineties there's no way to stop, short of winning the sweepstakes or succumbing to a full-blown nervous breakdown. Since one is unlikely and the other unhealthy, we need to apply the brakes to our busy lives.

Sometimes a woman's place *is* in a restaurant. Any restaurant. Sitting down and being served.

❊ AFFIRMATION:
I can afford an occasional treat.

The life which is unexamined is not worth living.

—*Plato*

Self-examination is a built-in safeguard against indispensability.

When we look honestly at ourselves, we're on the road to recovery. We begin to see how, when, and why we use indispensability to run away from emptiness and bribe others for love.

It can be frightening to face the truth, because it shows us important changes we may not be ready to make. It's fine to go slowly, to unearth only as much information as feels right.

 AFFIRMATION:
I am ready to know myself.

Since I was twenty-four . . . there never was any vagueness in my plans or ideas as to what God's work was for me.

—Florence Nightingale

Some people know their calling at age nine, while others, well into their thirties, are still trying to figure out what to do when they grow up.

Indispensable Women tend to push the river along, rather than letting it flow. We make one-year, five-year, even twenty-year plans in an effort to feel on top of our lives. We set rigid goals and stick to them come hell or high water.

But the course curves. We need to remain flexible and open to constant reevaluation in order to make the right choice, right now, in the present.

❧ AFFIRMATION:
I can change my mind.

Blessed art Thou, O God . . . who has commanded us to kindle the Sabbath light.

—Jewish liturgy

In the Jewish tradition, the Sabbath—or Shabbat—is a time set aside for rest and study. No work is allowed; cooking, carrying, and all other forms of labor are forbidden from sunset Friday to sunset Saturday.

Although I do not observe Shabbat to the letter of the law, the idea of a twenty-four-hour period devoted to quiet, reflective time is very appealing. How wonderful to *have* to rest. Jewish mystics call Shabbat "a foretaste of the world to come."

The idea of scheduling downtime—and sticking to it—makes sense for all Indispensable Women, whether by keeping the Sabbath or simply making time each day.

�֍ AFFIRMATION:
It is a blessing to rest.

Mourning is making peace with change.
                              —*Yakima Indian Nation*

I am going through a divorce. It is scary and painful; I find myself pushing through. Macho Mommy in survival mode, immersing myself in deadlines as if nothing has happened.

Finally I end up in the emergency room with a ten-day migraine that won't let up, even with a shot of Demerol. I can no longer work. My body breaks down so that I have to stop.

When I stop, I feel the depth of my loss. I begin to grieve the end of my eleven-year marriage, weeping until the pain in my head moves to my heart, where it belongs.

When I finish this round of mourning, I am able to work again.

❁ **AFFIRMATION:**
My indispensability won't relieve my pain, it will only prolong it.

> *I did not have three thousand pairs of shoes, I had one thousand and sixty.*
>
> —Imelda Marcos

Funny, but sad. We may not be able to imagine owning quite that many shoes, but we *do* know what it's like to go to extremes in an attempt to "fix" our feelings.

We binge on sugar, exercise compulsively, or shop till we drop. The more we put out, the more we need to find ways to stay "up" and reward ourselves for our efforts.

But nothing is enough. All the shoes in the Philippines won't heel (whoops, heal) the pain beneath our indispensability. We need to break the pattern, not find solace in false sources of support.

❈ AFFIRMATION:
I know that I feed my indispensability with other compulsive behavior. Any time I am ready, I can stop.

#8. Clean dresser drawers in case of a fire.

—*I.W. seminar*

We prepare for calamity because it makes us feel in control. Putting our affairs in order creates a semblance of security, even though we know, rationally, that fires and other calamities are usually beyond our control.

There's another option: to anticipate the inevitable storms of life with serenity rather than battening the hatches for the worst-case scenario.

 **AFFIRMATION:**
Some things are out of my control.

My ex-husband used to say to me, "You look ugly. Ahh, now that I have your attention . . ." He said when he complimented me, I never heard him, but as soon as he said something negative, I perked right up.

—Natalie Goldberg

When someone compliments us, we brace ourselves for the bad news—an insult or qualifying statement to take the edge off our good feelings.

Our selective perception makes it easy to take in (and believe) negative feedback while filtering out what's positive. We do so in order to protect ourselves—"I'll say all the bad stuff to myself before anyone else does!"

Loving ourselves is a daily discipline. It is a process of unconditionally affirming our accomplishments without qualifying them in any way. Without waiting for the other shoe to drop.

✿ AFFIRMATION:
I dare to feel good about myself.

Concern should drive us into action and not into a depression.

—Karen Horney

We feel deeply the needs of our friends, family, and community; just waking up and reading the newspaper is more than enough to make us depressed.

Action is the antidote to despair. We aren't effective when paralyzed by feelings of overresponsibility. We need to act purposefully, trusting that each step we take can make a difference.

This *doesn't* mean taking on the world. Our only task is to know who we are and do what we can.

❀ AFFIRMATION:
I can help.

Where there is too much, something is missing.
                                    —Jewish saying

Our indispensability drives us to excess—we try too
hard, work too much; rigid determination wins the
day, but exacts a handsome price in other parts of our
lives.

Balance is the end goal of recovery. Work without
rest, action without receptivity wear us down and
wear us out.

All parts of ourselves must be nourished in order to
lead a balanced life.

❧ AFFIRMATION:
I will give equal attention to my body, mind, and
heart.

I don't know the key to success, but the key to failure is trying to please everyone.

—*Bill Cosby*

There's no way in the world to please everyone, although Indispensable Women try mightily. We can't stand for anyone to be disappointed because we're afraid of losing their love.

If we put a priority on pleasing ourselves, we are bound to do the right thing.

Doing the right thing *doesn't* mean doing what makes other people happy. It means satisfying ourselves that we are making decisions in accordance with our ethics and values.

 **AFFIRMATION:**
I succeed when I'm true to myself.

> *I often want to cry. That is the only advantage women have over men—at least they can cry.*
>
> —Jean Rhys

We fight our tears, struggling to be strong even when a good cry is exactly what we need.

For Indispensable Women, crying may seem like a waste of time. More than once I've watched women who are hurting stiffen their shoulders, take a deep breath, and carry on like good, dry-eyed soldiers. I want to send them a tape of Barbara Walters's interview with General Norman Schwarzkopf who said, tears in his eyes, "I'd worry about any general who couldn't cry."

Crying is cleansing. Watch what happens when children bawl; afterward they're spent but peaceful, then comes a new burst of energy.

❄ AFFIRMATION:
My tears are worth my time.

Housekeeping ain't no joke!

—Louisa May Alcott

Most Indispensable Women aim for "house beautiful." Those lavish magazine layouts of designer rooms with perfectly matched throw pillows lying just so on lavishly upholstered couches conspire to make us feel guilty if we're not proving our Superwoman status in the traditional way. We feel antsy amid piles of stuff, guilty knowing that dust lurks in the corners of our lived-in living rooms, compelled to create a pristine and sparkling atmosphere.

In fact, nobody cares, except ourselves. Better that our home is comfortable than a showplace for other people's pleasure.

❋ AFFIRMATION:
My house is a home, not a magazine layout.

When you stop making yourself indispensable, you get more done. You stop squandering your energy and running around in circles.

—The Indispensable Woman

Ironically, the more we do, the less we get done. As we spread ourselves thin, we stop paying quality attention. We make sloppy mistakes and forget the point of what we're doing, because our brains are worn out.

Indispensable Woman Recovery Lesson #3: Less is more. The goal of recovery is to home in on the things that matter most. Then we can focus our energy. Then we're satisfied by a job well done.

�֍ AFFIRMATION:
It's quality, not quantity, that counts.

No Pampers, Pampering: A cushy camp for moms.
                              —Newsweek *magazine headline,*
                                              July 1989

Two resourceful women in California came up with a
hot idea: summer camp for moms—and not the sleep-
in-a-tent variety, either. Oh no. These are pampered
campers. Champagne on check-in. Gourmet meals.
Massage and other indulgences for Indispensable
Women totally deserving of "Queen for a Day" perks.

   I read this article and had two thoughts: 1. Why
didn't I think of this? 2. Where do I sign up?

❀ **AFFIRMATION:**
I qualify for royal treatment.

If I'm such a legend, then why am I so lonely?
                                                    —Judy Garland

It's sobering to think of the superstars who burned brightly, then burned out.

Judy Garland, Janis Joplin, Marilyn Monroe—big-time Indispensable Women—touched millions of lives, yet died all alone.

Ours is a smaller stage, yet we experience similar isolation when we trade indispensability for intimacy.

It's one thing to wow them. But when the curtain falls, we're alone in the spotlight.

❀ AFFIRMATION:
Today I will take a day off from dazzling anyone.

I don't want to belong to any club that would accept me as a member.

—Groucho Marx

Grandiosity and low self-esteem are two sides of the same coin. Our self-image is distorted; we swing back and forth between self-deception—"I'm best at everything"—and self-deprecation—"I have nothing to offer."

Both are false. Recovery from indispensability requires seeing ourselves as just enough—neither too much nor too little.

When we step down from godliness and accept our humanity, we are able to experience equal give-and-take. No leader, no follower, simply human beings walking side by side.

❋ AFFIRMATION:
I can have the pleasure of being a peer.

Some of my feelings have been stored so long they have freezer burn.

—Melody Beattie

We freeze our feelings because we're too frightened and vulnerable to deal with them. We learn to carry on, acting as if everything were just fine.

When we're ready, we slowly thaw them out. It takes time, trust, and safety to face feelings from the past. Out in the open, little by little, the pain melts away.

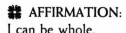 AFFIRMATION:
I can be whole.

My husband said he wanted to have a relationship with a redhead, so I dyed my hair red.

—Jane Fonda

What lengths we go to, to fit other people's fantasies!

In my mid-thirties, I experimented with short hair, wild hair, streaked hair, in search of a new look.

One day I went to the beauty shop for a perm. I ended up with a hair intervention. My colorist looked deeply into my eyes and said: "I really care about you and I really care about your hair. If you perm it, it will fall out." Next, my stylist showed up, earnestly pleading with me to give up my old, wild-maned image of myself. The shampooist chimed in, and then the manicurist. "Okay, okay!" I caved in under the collective concern. "But if you won't perm it, color it."

❀ **AFFIRMATION:**
I will look good for myself.

The opposite of talking isn't listening. The opposite of talking is waiting.

—*Fran Lebowitz*

Indispensable Women finish other people's sentences. Why wait when we know what they're thinking?

Not only do we not listen well, we jump in before it's our turn. It's not because we're rude; it's because we're so anxious to be heard. We're desperate to show off how much we know and convince others of our winning point of view.

Being respectful—which requires listening with an open mind and open heart—is more important and more rewarding than being right.

❀ AFFIRMATION:
I can wait my turn.

> *I followed my employees around, rearranging the books on the shelves. Once I slept on a sleeping bag in the storeroom.*
> —*Bookstore manager at an I.W. seminar*

We just can't let go! Instead of letting other people do their jobs, we supermanage—redoing or suggesting ever better ways to get things done.

Perfectionism prevents us from being effective at helping other people grow. It's the difference between being a manager and being a leader: Managers get the work done even if it means stepping on toes. Leaders guide in an effort to bring out the best.

❈ AFFIRMATION:
I will resist the temptation to run the show.

> *One of the symptoms of approaching nervous breakdown is the belief that one's work is terribly important.*
> —Bertrand Russell

It's a paradox—on the one hand, we must see the value in our work; on the other hand, we mustn't take it too seriously.

Keeping work in perspective keeps us sane. What I do matters. YES! Will the world turn without it? Also yes.

Anxiety kicks in when we pressure ourselves to produce something of monumental importance, when we put too much stake in our work.

The Zen phrase *right livelihood* instructs us to see our vocation as an integral part of the universe. Everyone's contribution is equal. The artist, farmer, merchant, and teacher each give something of importance.

❀ AFFIRMATION:
My work isn't worth a nervous breakdown.

Let the world know you as you are, not as you think you should be, because sooner or later, if you are posing, you will forget the pose, and then where are you?

—Fanny Brice

In our self-consciousness we create a facade—a carefully designed mask that hides our real selves.

After a while, we forget who we really are. We buy our own act, believing the version of reality we've sold to the world.

Recovering our authentic selves means peeling away the layers of artifice covering our fear. If we remove the mask, what will we see? How will others react?

In a moment of courage, see yourself in the mirror. Look deeply into your own eyes and say:

❀ **AFFIRMATION:**
I am me. That's all I have to be.

So little time, so little to do.

—*Oscar Levant*

First we heave a big, drawn-out sigh. Followed by a laugh.

What a twist on our usual way of thinking about our lives! The joke is on us: There's *lots* of time, and, despite our normal frantic pace, there's not as much to do as we think.

Time is relative. Forty-five minutes to ourselves on a Sunday afternoon flies by. Forty-five minutes on the runway waiting for engine repair seems an eternity.

It's up to us to make the most of our time. And to stop living as if the meter were running.

❊ AFFIRMATION:
It will all get done.

I want to be able to live without a crowded calendar. I want to be able to read a book without feeling guilty or go to a concert when I like. . . .

—*Golda Meir*

We yearn for time to idle away. For the luxury of lazy afternoons spent reading and dreaming.

Instead, even recreation is squeezed between other appointments. We're always coming from somewhere, on the way to somewhere else.

If there was an Indispensable Woman Gift Certificate, it would read: "Four hours uninterrupted time. Do anything you please."

❀ AFFIRMATION:

I am in charge of my calendar. It's up to me to leave spaces of open time.

The best remedy for those who are afraid, lonely, or unhappy is to go outside, somewhere where they can be quite alone with the heavens, nature, and God.

—*Anne Frank*

I get trapped within prison walls of my own making—deadlines, business calls, housecleaning that won't wait—forgetting that fresh air and blossoming crab apple trees lie right outside my door.

Nothing calms me quite so much as standing at the edge of the breathtaking marsh right across the street. It's like being inside a gorgeous painting, personally signed by God.

My fears are quieted when my feet are firmly on the ground, my gaze set on the horizon. I breathe, gratefully look around me, and return to work.

AFFIRMATION:
It's right outside my front door.

. . . but it does *move!*

—*Galileo*

Rumor has it these were the famous astronomer's last words.

So often we doubt our own perceptions. We're sure it's black, but when everyone else sees white, we rub our eyes or adjust our glasses to conform with the majority opinion.

We think that indispensability rests on agreeing with everyone. That reinforcing other people's viewpoint endears us to them forever.

Not so. Seeing what we see and saying what that is —even if it's controversial—wins far greater respect.

❀ **AFFIRMATION:**
I trust myself.

Each of us, fundamentally, is separate and alone—a reality most people grapple with daily and find difficult to accept.
—The Indispensable Woman

We fight this by surrounding ourselves with people who depend on us. Relationships—which we secure by making ourselves indispensable—ease the terror of solitude.

What happens when those around us aren't so needy? When friends are doing fine, when our children grow increasingly independent?

It's nice to be needed, but it's nicer to know that our friends and children choose our company because they love us, not because they can't live without us.

❊ AFFIRMATION:
When I am with myself, I am not alone.

> *Do I contradict myself? Very well then I contradict myself. (I am large, I contain multitudes.)*
>
> —*Walt Whitman*

Indispensable Women are uncomfortable with contradictions. Inconsistency is troubling; we need objective reality, landmarks, so as to know exactly where we are.

But nothing stands still. Acceptance of contradiction is the foundation of growth and change. It's uncomfortable, but it's also what makes life interesting.

As we do grow and change, we become more complex, more vital. One day we're sure of who we are; the next day we discover whole new layers as we continue to emerge.

❀ AFFIRMATION:
There are many sides of me.

It's not true that life is one damn thing after another—it's one damn thing over and over.

—Edna St. Vincent Millay

We keep making the same mistakes until we get it right. Each time, we get a little closer, a little more aware of who we are and why we do what we do.

It's frustrating to keep tramping over the same ground again and again. To keep getting tripped up. Sometimes we wonder whether we're getting anywhere.

The next time you run up against a recurring pattern—an old, familiar anxiety attack, or the same old fight you repeatedly have with your mother—notice how much more quickly you see what's going on. Notice how quickly you get beyond it.

❊ AFFIRMATION:
I am making progress.

> *The* vacuum *automatically sweeps up whatever is in her path. Her work load expands to include whatever isn't being taken care of.*
>
> —The Indispensable Woman

Rather than discriminating—saying yes to some things, no to others—we simply do what's in front of us. We plow through the house, gathering up yesterday's socks and underwear instead of leaving them for the children to put in the hamper. When the phone rings, we answer *and* talk, even if it's a friend calling smack in the middle of dinner.

Sometimes we need to turn off the vacuum, even when the path is littered with unfinished tasks. This is an exercise in surrender, to say to ourselves:

❋ AFFIRMATION:
The rest will have to wait.

After all, tomorrow is another day.
                        —*Scarlett O'Hara,* Gone with the Wind

We have second chances. We make progress *and* we make mistakes, which are valuable if we learn from them and move on.

A young manager from a multinational corporation was hired to direct the two-year start-up of a new division. The project failed and the dispirited director went to his vice president to resign. "No way," she said, "after we just spent two years and three million dollars educating you?"

Slips (let's hope they don't all have a three-million-dollar price tag) are permissible! We miss the mark and fall back into old patterns, but we needn't stay stuck in guilt and recrimination.

Tomorrow brings an invitation: to recommit to recovery.

�֍ AFFIRMATION:
I have lots of chances.

> *The heaviest burdens in life are the things that might hap-*
> *pen but don't.*
>
> —*Anonymous*

Make a quick list of everything on your mind. Now, put an X next to anything that falls into the category of *anticipated stress*.

Chances are good that at least 50 percent of what burdens you hasn't, and probably won't, come to pass. My list includes: finding a raccoon in the shower, forgetting to pay the mortgage, getting hit by a car so I can't finish this book.

Lighten your load by taking the *anticipated stress* category and dropping it overboard.

❄ AFFIRMATION:
If it's going to happen, it will.

It is not enough for us to be busy . . . the question is: what are we busy about?

—Henry David Thoreau

Being busy—just for the sake of being busy—is a waste of our precious time. We distract ourselves but achieve little of value.

By contrast, purposeful activity is deeply satisfying. We know what we're doing and why. In the end, aimless busyness exhausts us, while purposeful activity reenergizes.

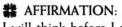 **AFFIRMATION:**
I will think before I act.

The author—a recovering Indispensable Woman—took today off. This one's yours. Silently or on the page, create your own meditation based on:

 **AFFIRMATION:**
Today I am free to do whatever I want.

Love does not consist in gazing at each other but in look-ing outward together in the same direction.

—Antoine de Saint-Exupery

We fall in love with falling in love. The experience of merging is intoxicating; we lose ourselves yet again in order to sustain the rush.

Love born of dependency is doomed. In our indispensability, we warm to this most passionate project. At last! A willing subject for boundless devotion! Someone to love and need me forever!

Lasting love consists of separateness. Not two halves that make a whole, but two whole people, each strengthened by the other.

❉ AFFIRMATION:
I will love myself first.

#17: Leave Gary a note reminding him to call his mother.
Leave Gary a note reminding him to read the first note.

                                        —*I.W. seminar*

It's profoundly disrespectful to treat our mates like morons.

We patronize and infantalize them, then wonder why they act like big babies.

We have to stop running the show. Start with the little things: Get out of the way while he folds the laundry or lines up a baby-sitter. *Don't* tell him how to do it, and *don't* criticize the results. Keep at this.

❈ **AFFIRMATION:**
I'm not his mother.

If I'm too strong for some people, that's their problem!
—*Glenda Jackson*

Maybe, but it *feels* like our problem. When others back away, threatened by our power, *we* end up hurt and alone.

This is a tough one! We mustn't water ourselves down in order to be more palatable; at the same time we must be careful not to wear a neon sign that flashes: STAY AWAY. I'M SO STRONG I DON'T NEED ANYONE.

We are powerful. We are soft. Both are our strengths.

❧ AFFIRMATION:
I am strong enough to be soft.

There is no shortage of good days. It is good lives that are hard to come by.

—*Annie Dillard*

How do you feel at the end of the day? Do you fall asleep with the sweet satisfaction of having lived another day to its fullest?

Making choices that make for a meaningful life—a life that reflects who we really are, a life that we can be proud of—is a constant and conscious pursuit.

Each day we make choices that cumulatively add up to a life. I choose to write because it's important to express myself. I choose to play with my children because being their mother matters.

Intentional choices turn good days into good lives.

❀ **AFFIRMATION:**
My life is of my own making.

Living with a saint is more grueling than being one.
                                        —*Robert Neville*

The irony is, Indispensable Women strive for saint-hood in order to secure our place in this world. But the strategy backfires. In the company of mere mortals, our goodness is more grueling than godly.

It is our humanness than makes us lovable. And bearable!

❈ **AFFIRMATION:**
Who can live with a saint?

If at first you don't succeed, read the directions.
                                        —*Anonymous*

We think everything should be a snap. That we should get it the first time and get it right, without even reading the directions.

Guidance is there for a reason. Whether it's pointers from a friend or step-by-step details on assembling your six-year-old's science kit, *accept it!*

Instructions are a concrete form of support, generally proven by experience. They help us get from Point A to Point B with the least effort and the best outcome. Why reinvent the wheel?

❈ AFFIRMATION:
I won't throw away the directions.

Life is what happens when you are making other plans.
                                            —John Lennon

I imagine John Lennon pausing in front of the Dakota to give his final, fatal autograph.

Dead at forty, his words and music are imprinted in the consciousness of millions. A song comes on the radio with a clear reminder that life is fleeting; if we spend our days making other plans, we may never see them realized.

How would John Lennon have spent his last hours had he been able to plan them? How would you spend yours?

❆ AFFIRMATION:
Life is happening right this minute.

Inspiration does not come like a bolt, nor is it kinetic energy striving, but it comes to us slowly and quietly and all the time. . . .

—Brenda Euland

When I was writing my first book, *Expecting Change*, I asked a fellow writer: How do you know the difference between stopping work in order to replenish the source, and quitting because you're just sick of the whole damn thing?

She said it was intuitive, something you learn, something that can't be taught.

Over the years, I've come to recognize the signs. When a deadline is looming and I *will* myself to create, I end up with fingernail marks in the palm of my hand. That means stop. Time to nap or have lunch with a friend. Simply avoiding work, on the other hand, is a sign of fear. If I'm frightened, it's time to slowly and quietly push through.

❀ AFFIRMATION:
It will come.

I gave birth to triplets. Three identical girls. I insisted on nursing all three. A few months ago, the littlest one died. I was so intent on being an Indispensable Mother, I never got to know my child.

—*I.W. seminar participant*

It is with the greatest intentions that we make ourselves indispensable. Love. Concern. Commitment to be the best mother, the best daughter, the best friend in the world.

But the best intentions won't give us back our health. Or the people we failed to really know because we didn't realize the difference between loving and letting go.

It's a huge price to pay.

❈ AFFIRMATION:
I am sorry.

If I didn't start painting, I would have raised chickens.
                                        —Grandma Moses

It's reassuring to know we have options. That we aren't cornered by doing any one thing, even when we're exceptionally good at it.

Believing we have lots of choices frees us to be more relaxed in what we do. Each day we reevaluate. If it's still the right choice—tomorrow and the day after—fine. If not, we can go sailing or raise chickens, or for that matter, paint.

Until we try, we don't know what we're capable of. Or what might make us happy.

❊ AFFIRMATION:
There are lots of ways to go.

We don't stop playing because we grow old; we grow old because we stop playing.

—*Anonymous*

When my daughter was three months old, her father and I went off on a vacation and left her for ten days with my already well-into-their-seventies in-laws. Upon our return we expected to find them haggard and ready for a holiday themselves.

But when we walked in, there they were, sitting cross-legged on the kitchen floor, laughing and playing with Zoe as if they were thirty years younger. By all appearances, they had drunk from the fountain of youth.

❦ AFFIRMATION:
I am young enough to play.

I look forward to being older, when what you look like becomes less and less an issue and what you are is the point.
—Susan Sarandon

At my high school reunion, I was struck by how much more confident women seem than back when we were seventeen and eighteen years old. There were few signs of hair-twirling, skirt-tugging, or self-deprecating apologies for weight gain or zits. Ten years later, my former classmates seemed noticeably more at ease.

I've noticed the same thing as I've traveled the country—older women who trade their critical emphasis on outward appearance for a deeper appreciation of self. Perhaps as we age, we begin to wear our beauty from the inside out.

❧ AFFIRMATION:
I am getting better every day.

If a few lustful and erotic reveries make the housework go by "as in a dream," why not?

—*Nancy Friday*

As young girls, we watched TV commercials glamorizing housework: women happily humming, seemingly having orgasms from scrubbing the toilet.

Then we discovered the truth: Cleaning toilets is the pits. There is nothing glamorous about it, especially when we are down on our knees at midnight after putting in a long day's work.

If you hate doing housework, do whatever it takes to get it done. Put on a music video and dance while you're vacuuming. Invite a friend over to share a bottle of wine (or soda water) while you clean the refrigerator. Divide up the job with other members of the household.

Be creative. It will help make it go faster.

❁ AFFIRMATION:
It's all right to hate housework.

I try to live out a sense of ritual in my life . . . by my power to dream, to move out of realism, by exaltation.
—Anaïs Nin

Indispensable Women are entrenched in the real world, where responsibility rules.

For balance we need dreams, prayer, and ritual—whatever elevates us, whatever helps us get beyond the day-to-day grind.

"If my life gets any more real, I'll kill myself," says one Indispensable Woman. What she means is: I am tired of having to be so grown-up all the time.

I remind her to take long walks, to make time for worship, to reflect on the meaning of her life.

❀ AFFIRMATION:
Spiritual nourishment feeds the heart.

Be careful what you pray for.

—*Anonymous*

This has always been one of my favorite sayings. I like the suggestion that what we *think* we want isn't always what makes us happy.

I prayed for worldly success, and now I have way too much work to do. I prayed for an answer to my ailing marriage, and the answer forced my hand.

Now I'm praying for the courage to handle what I've been given.

 **AFFIRMATION:**
I am prepared to receive the answers to my prayers.

Do you wish other people would move faster?

—The Indispensable Woman

You can always tell an Indispensable Woman in a traffic jam; she's the one gunning the motor and tapping her fingers nervously on the dashboard.

We're always in a rush and we rush other people. We nag our children to hurry and get out the door; we barely hide our irritation as coworkers muse for several moments before responding to a question.

If everyone would just move a little faster, the world would be better off. Of course, there'd be more fender benders. More hurried children. More mistakes on the job . . .

AFFIRMATION:

Faster isn't always better.

I loafe and invite my soul,
I lean and loafe at my ease observing
A spear of summer grass

—*Walt Whitman*

Today I took a friend out to brunch for her birthday at the New French Café. She said her perfect day consisted of handing her beloved baby to her husband, reading the paper in bed, and spending hours doing whatever her heart desired.

Every woman needs—and deserves—at *least* one day a year just for ourselves. A day when we can hear the sound of our voice without negotiating with screaming children for a moment of peace. A day when we can happily loafe or walk through the door with the freedom to think solely of our own pleasure.

Being alone—giving ourselves a day off from taking care of other people—isn't selfish. It's necessary self-love.

❈ AFFIRMATION:
It's my turn.

Being popular is very important. Otherwise people might not like you.

—*Mimi Pond,* The Valley Girl's Guide

I love this! It makes me feel about fifteen years old, anxious and insecure, changing outfits twenty times in order to dress for a party.

We *do* want to be liked. To Indispensable Women, popularity is money in the bank. It guarantees us of always having someone to be with when we don't feel like being alone.

All of which is great. As long as we don't base our self-esteem on our popularity rating. As long as we look in the mirror and like what we see.

❀ AFFIRMATION:
It's nice to be liked. It's better to like myself.

To do is to be.

—*Socrates*

We get confused and think that what we *do* is who we *are*: Ellen Sue Stern—Author-Speaker-Mother-Friend-Community Volunteer.

But we exist not because of our accomplishments; our accomplishments exist because of who we are. Because of our values. Our spirit. Our individuality.

When we define our identity through our achievements, we limit and diminish ourselves. In truth, what we do is but a small part of who we are.

 AFFIRMATION:
I already am before I do anything.

To be is to do.

—*Plato*

We get confused and think that what we *are* is what we *do*: Ellen Sue Stern—only as good as her last accomplishment.

No! No! No! There is more to being than doing. Sitting silently by a stream or savoring a strawberry ice cream cone in steamy July is as much a part of life as anything else.

Just being able to be—without having to prove a thing—is more than enough to do.

❀ **AFFIRMATION:**
I needn't do anything to be.

I look at the way we have divided up the space in our house. My husband has a little space that is considered his own, and I have no space that is mine. It's as if I exist everywhere and nowhere.

—Our Bodies, Ourselves

Indispensable Women are all over the place, making life hospitable for our partners, our children, our friends. Yet we forget to secure a "room of our own," as Virginia Woolf so aptly put it.

We need to carve out time and space for ourselves. A piece of uninterrupted time in which *no one* is allowed to ask anything of us. A corner we claim in which to do exactly as we wish.

It's imperative to feel our separateness. To know that we are not invisible.

✿ AFFIRMATION:
I exist apart from everyone else.

The truly free woman is one who knows how to decline a dinner invitation without giving an excuse.

—*Anonymous*

As I was contemplating this quote, the phone rang. On the other end was a man I'd just met asking me to dinner. I didn't want to go; I wasn't in the mood for a date or particularly attracted to him.

So I said yes. I couldn't come up with any good reason to turn him down.

What's the worst that can happen if we decline? We'll hurt someone's feelings? They won't ask again? Sooner or later *everyone* will stop asking?

We aren't obligated to go places we don't want to be. So I'm picking up the phone. I'll simply say: "No, thank you."

❀ AFFIRMATION:
I don't owe anyone an explanation.

What about men? Aren't they indispensable?
                                    —*I.W. seminar participant*

I have met few men who make themselves indispensable. Workaholic, yes. Codependent, perhaps in certain areas of their lives.

But men, in general, are different from women in two important ways: (1) They define themselves according to far fewer roles (husband, father, worker, golfer . . .) and are clearer about their focus and priorities. (2) Men aren't the caretakers that women are. They're less likely to feel responsible for other people's feelings and needs.

In the extreme, women are overly caring, while men are overly detached. The ideal lies somewhere in between.

✿ AFFIRMATION:
We can learn from each other.

Happiness is a habit—cultivate it.

—*Elbert Hubbard*

Indispensability is habit-forming. We work hard at it every single day.

Yet we expect happiness just to happen (or not happen) depending on our mood. We think it's a by-product rather than a predictable part of life.

Like everything else, happiness takes effort. Or, at the very least, a belief in its possibility. We have the power to create, cultivate, and count on it.

✿ AFFIRMATION:
Today I will make sure to do at least one thing that makes me happy.

Don't compromise yourself. You are all you've got.
—Janis Joplin

When we compromise ourselves—by hedging, capitulating, or failing to fight for what we believe in—a little piece of ourselves caves in. It's a slippery slope; first we give in on the little things; before long we've given up our voice and our vote.

Compromise and compromising ourselves are two different things. The one involves honoring ourselves; the other involves failing ourselves.

 AFFIRMATION:
I will keep myself intact.

Sometimes I wonder if men and women really suit each other. Perhaps they should live next door and just visit now and then.

—Katharine Hepburn

I wonder too. Sometimes it seems as if we were alien species in dire need of an interpreter.

In her recent bestseller, *You Just Don't Understand,* author and linguist Deborah Tannen points out how differently women and men communicate. Indispensable Women are easily frustrated by how hard it is to decipher the code.

Bridging the language barrier takes patience and effort. We hear better when we stop talking—when we listen.

❄ AFFIRMATION:
When I'm frustrated, it's better to stop.

Whatever doesn't kill you makes you strong.

—*Goethe*

The hardest lessons are the greatest teachers.

Family scars, lost loves, career crossroads, and life crises force us to tap into our deepest pools of courage and power.

When faced with difficulties, we have a choice: to become embattled and embittered, or to muster our forces and find new depths of strength.

❊ AFFIRMATION:
I welcome every experience as a way to grow.

Don't hurry, don't worry. You're only here for a short visit.

—*Anonymous*

We set foot in exotic places with heightened awareness, our senses open to the sights, sounds, and smells.

What if we led our everyday lives the same way? Waking each morning like visitors in a foreign land, eager for discovery?

Our time here is so brief; we get the most out of it when we travel with a spirit of adventure.

❊ AFFIRMATION:
This is a great trip.

We don't see things as they are, we see things as we are.
—*Anaïs Nin*

We think that the way we see things is the way they *are*, when in fact, our perception is highly subjective —refracted by the thick lens of our life experience.

We are nearsighted by nature because we see from behind our own two eyes. We're attached to our familiar picture of reality and have trouble with alternative interpretations.

True 20/20 vision requires seeing things through other people's eyes as well.

AFFIRMATION:
My vision is clear.

Question: *How many Indispensable Women does it take to change a lightbulb?*

Answer: *Three. One to write detailed instructions. One to change the lightbulb. And one to make sure it's done right.*
                              —The Indispensable Woman

How complicated is it?

We approach each task with equal intensity, even when it's as straightforward as changing a lightbulb.

Not everything merits such detailed attention. Let's save our energy for the big things. How many Indispensable Women does it take to change a lightbulb? One. And it only takes a minute.

❄ AFFIRMATION:
I can control my intensity.

I hate women because they always know where things are.
                                        —*James Thurber*

Indispensable Women would really annoy him! Even when we can't find our keys, we exude competence. We've got a system. Knowing where things are—even if they're not where they're supposed to be—is how I.W.'s cope in order to manage all the details.

Gary gets furious when he's frantically foraged for forty-five minutes looking for Evan's library book and I casually reach up and retrieve it from the top of the fridge.

Organization is helpful as long as it makes life easier.

❋ AFFIRMATION:
I can find it.

What lies before us and what lies beyond us is tiny compared to what lies within us.

—*Henry David Thoreau*

Indispensable Women look outside for fulfillment. We seek meaning by immersing ourselves in work, relationships, and other activities.

While searching high and low for external validation, we neglect to look within. We forget to mine the rich vein of love, wisdom, and creativity we inherently possess.

This is an exercise in tapping your inner resources: Close your eyes. Be perfectly silent. Picture yourself as a shell. Now an ocean. Now a universe.

❈ AFFIRMATION:
I am a world unto myself.

Perhaps someday it will be pleasant to remember even this.
—*Virgil*

Much of what we face is difficult. Sickness, financial pressure, trials in friendship and love cast a pall over our day-to-day lives.

Only in retrospect does suffering make sense. Looking back, we know the strength of character derived from getting through hard times and coming out on the other side.

Here's where Indispensable Women have the edge: We are adept at making lemonade from lemons—allow time to bring its sweetness to the bitter.

✽ AFFIRMATION:
There's a reason for everything.

Hot fudge fills deep needs.

—*Susan Isaacs*

I am sitting in the Lowry Café, working against the clock, eating double chocolate soufflé cake.

When we push ourselves too hard, we end up angry and tired. We soothe ourselves with "comfort food" as a baby reaches for her mother's breast.

But the sweetness is short-lived. Our sugar high gives way, and we plunge into a deep well of sadness for which grieving, not goodies, is the answer.

❈ **AFFIRMATION:**
Feeling our feelings fills deep needs.

Is it necessary to have read Spinoza in order to make out a laundry list?

—Jean Detourbey

I have a friend, Rachel, who uses big words. Words with twelve and thirteen letters, that I have to look up in the dictionary later.

Sometimes I'm intimidated by her. Like most Indispensable Women, I am competitive; when someone knows something I don't, I feel as if there were something wrong with me.

In fact, Rachel and I have a great deal to learn from each other. When I remember that, it becomes a pleasure to expand my vocabulary. I am able to be both teacher and student.

❀ AFFIRMATION:
I become more when I am not afraid of being less.

Neurosis seems to be a human privilege.

—*Sigmund Freud*

We analyze ourselves to death—probing our psyches under microscopic scrutiny.

We would do well to let up on this endless self-examination, to live life without constantly questioning our motivations—saving therapy for serious issues.

Not everything is deeply meaningful. The sun shines because it shines, not because it had a happy childhood.

AFFIRMATION:

Having issues to work on doesn't make me neurotic.

#4: Finish next week's work so I don't get behind.
—I.W. seminar

We counter our fear of falling behind by working way ahead of schedule.

This is one clear area of self-imposed stress. Although it temporarily eases anxiety, pushing the deadlines doesn't really provide breathing room; we find more work to fill in the empty slots.

Our pace needn't be controlled by fear. We need to do only what must be done today.

❀ AFFIRMATION:
I can slow down and still succeed.

*May God defend me from my friends: I can defend myself
from my enemies.*

—*Voltaire*

We give the world to our close friends and demand
the same in return. When they disappoint us, we
question their loyalty.

Writer Anna Quindlen elaborates: "I expect my
women friends to love me unconditionally, to understand me when I'm sobbing and be able to tell me
why the meat thermometer isn't supposed to touch
the bone."

Give me a break! Instead of reinforcing the Superwoman setup, it's time for women to support one another. The last thing we need is pressure from our
friends!

✿ **AFFIRMATION:**
I will be easier on myself and my friends.

Appreciation: A gesture, word, or act has shown forth and, like a warm wave of light, has moved our heart.

—I Ching

We take ourselves for granted.

Each time we send forth our "warm waves of light," it's essential to pause and appreciate the effort. For playing catch with our children—Thank you. For finishing a challenging project, for visiting an aging relative—Thank you. For spending three hours listening to a friend—Thank you.

Every gesture, word, or act of gratitude goes a long way. Appreciation is a form of love. We begin by giving it to ourselves.

❀ AFFIRMATION:
I am worthy of appreciation.

This too shall pass.

—*Shakespeare*

At the height of a crisis, in the heat of the moment, we lose all perspective. We can't imagine when or how things will ever get back to normal.

Given enough time, most crises pass. Until then, we can make life easier by watching our tendency toward drama, by keeping in mind that even the hottest fires eventually burn themselves out.

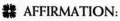 **AFFIRMATION:**
This too shall pass.

And the trouble is, if you don't risk anything, you risk even more.

—Erica Jong

We are brave. We are gutsy. But perfectionism stifles how deep we are able to go.

We take calculated risks: one toe in, testing the waters. But diving is risky. The temperature has to be *just* right.

When we stop at the surface, we limit the richest possibilities. Unimaginable beauty lies at the bottom of the sea.

 AFFIRMATION:
I can dive in without drowning.

Just remember, we're all in this alone.

—*Lily Tomlin*

This is the beauty and the sorrow of life: that we are intimately connected, yet ultimately alone.

Indispensable Women struggle to figure out the difference between independence, dependence, and interdependence.

The first means we can stand on our own two feet. The second means we hold each other up. The third means we walk together, hand in hand.

❀ AFFIRMATION:
I can lean on other people without losing myself.

I am still learning.

—Michelangelo

From birth to death we are learning; the more we know, the more there is to know. At no point along the way should we expect ourselves to have arrived. There is nothing to prove. No final exam. Indispensable Women don't need graduate degrees to be knowledgeable; a truly open mind is the only requirement.

✿ AFFIRMATION:
Today I learned _____.

*Do you jump up and do the dishes or answer the phone
before anyone else has a chance? Have you given your friends
carte blanche to call on you when they need you, without
spelling out any conditions?*

—The Indispensable Woman

We set ourselves up. Now it's time to set some limits.

It's even okay to change the rules. Say you're sick
of doing the dishes every night.

Try paper plates. Or delegate. Even a carefully
trained six-year-old can wash a dish.

Your friends will love you even if your "office
hours" are strictly nine to five. *You get to protect your time
and energy.* Friends who can't respect limits aren't
friends.

❋ AFFIRMATION:
I made myself indispensable. I can unmake myself
indispensable.

> *Try to love the questions themselves, as if they were locked rooms or books written in a very foreign language.*
> —Rainer Maria Rilke

We want the answers, when the questions themselves are more engaging.

Having answers makes us feel secure. If we can answer the pressing questions—Who am I? What shall I do with my life?—then our uncertainty is lessened.

But answers are ephemeral; they slide through our fingers like mercury from a shattered thermometer. Who am I? Someone different than I was yesterday. What shall I do with my life? The question takes on new shades of meaning as we peel away the layers of ourselves.

❧ AFFIRMATION:
I have all the questions. I needn't have all the answers.

I've been on a constant diet for the past two decades. I've lost a total of 789 pounds. By all accounts, I should be hanging from a charm bracelet.

—*Erma Bombeck*

We diet zealously, living on celery sticks and miracle concoctions. We do it in order to be pretty. Sexy. Desirable. We do it because we're uncomfortable in our own skin.

At times our perfectionism leads to serious harm. We diet until we're weak and dehydrated, or binge and purge in a desperate, self-destructive cycle.

If you're not sure whether you've crossed the line, ask a friend or counselor. And *listen!*

❧ AFFIRMATION:
Looking good isn't worth killing myself over.

No one steps into the same river twice.

—Heraclitus

Nothing stays the same. Like the river, our lives are a living stream of movement and change.

Like the river, too, we must keep moving on, allowing ourselves to be who we are, make mistakes, and begin anew.

❀ AFFIRMATION:
Every moment is a new beginning.

Not only is there no God, try getting a plumber on the weekend.

—*Woody Allen*

Is there a God? Or isn't there? And does it matter?

Indispensable Women want guarantees. We hate to invest in the plan without an acclaimed architect and foolproof blueprints.

Here's where faith comes in. We must live our lives assured they have meaning, praising the universe, with or without *a priori* proof of God's presence.

 **AFFIRMATION:**
This is the mystery. This is the magic.

The one important thing I have learned over the years is the difference between taking one's work seriously and taking one's self seriously. The first is imperative and the second disastrous.

—Margot Fonteyn

A friend of mine, Tom Olson, whose birthday is today, showed me this quotation. It's perfect for Indispensable Women.

It's good to throw ourselves wholeheartedly into our work, to make a passionate commitment.

At the same time, we mustn't take ourselves too seriously. High expectations promote excellence; grandiosity creates undue pressure and strips work of its joy.

❀ AFFIRMATION:
I can shoot for the stars and keep my feet on the ground.

I put in sixteen-hour shifts in the intensive care unit. By the end of the day I feel like a hollow shell.

—*I.W. seminar participant*

Taking care of others, especially in emergency settings, gets our adrenaline pumping. It's a rush to be needed—the more desperately the better.

I know a woman who worked three jobs, was in graduate school, volunteered at church, and cared for her aging father, who lived with her. When I met her, she had just been released from the hospital where she'd had an emergency appendectomy.

Eventually our bodies give out. We think we're operating in a high-energy jet stream, but we stress ourselves so badly, we end up crashing to the ground.

❈ **AFFIRMATION:**
I will keep some for myself.

*People make their own world; at least a lot of them do.
You gotta take what comes. If it isn't what you want, it's
probably something you deserve.*

—Dorothy Molter

Dorothy Molter lived alone in a cabin in northern
Minnesota. She sold homemade root beer to thou-
sands of wilderness travelers canoeing through the
Boundary Waters.

We can do anything we want. We can be artists,
corporate executives, and then one day give it all up
and go live in the woods.

For five years I worked as heir apparent at my parents' publishing company. After much soul-searching,
I walked away, terrified at what I was losing, but
knowing in my heart it would never be mine.

It was the right decision. But in the moment, that
isn't necessarily evident. We have to learn to trust our
gut feelings.

❀ AFFIRMATION:
When I'm honest with myself, I know what I need
to do.

> *The motto should not be, Forgive one another; rather,*
> *Understand one another.*
>
> —*Anonymous*

Indispensable Women are the caretakers of relationships. Sometimes, in our effort to orchestrate intimacy, we create discord. We hurt our partners and then feel paralyzed by shame.

Making amends is part of recovery: "I'm sorry I pushed you." "I apologize for thinking I knew how you felt. Forgive me."

Beyond forgiveness is empathy. Mutual understanding is fostered when we can say:

❄ AFFIRMATION:
I am me. You are you. We are different but equal.

Hope for a miracle. But don't depend on one.

—*Talmud*

Hope mixed with hard work is the best recipe for getting what we want out of life.

Personally, I enter every sweepstakes. I tear open the envelope, choose between the red BMW and the blue sailboat, and race for the mailbox to qualify for the time-limited million-dollar bonus. And I *always* order magazines that the sweepstakes are intended to sell. I'm convinced they conveniently "lose" the ones with the "Thank You, Not Ordering" labels, even though they insist you don't have to order to win.

Meanwhile I continue to hammer away at my work. Maybe I'll get lucky. Maybe I already am.

 AFFIRMATION:
I'm depending on myself.

> *Guilt is the price we pay willingly for doing what we are going to do anyway.*
>
> —*Isabelle Holland*

If we're going to do it anyway, then why can't we just skip making ourselves miserable?

Maybe guilt is a choice; maybe it serves a necessary purpose in the grand scheme of our psyches.

Perhaps guilt is necessary reparation to make book with ourselves: *We fail. We pay. We're even.*

Where does this equation come from? How about: *I failed. I'm sorry. It's done.*

 **AFFIRMATION:**
I can choose to let go of my guilt.

If I only had a little humility, I would be perfect.
—*Ted Turner*

If Ted Turner had humility, we might not have CNN.

Humility is useful as long as it inspires us to greater things and makes us more grateful for what we have.

Humility is *not* the opposite of hubris. It is pride that knows its place.

❁ AFFIRMATION:
True humility requires an appreciation of my gifts.

> *People use words like "anxiety attack," as if anxiety is out there and attacks you.*
>
> —*Wayne W. Dyer*

Anxiety is the Indispensable Woman's shadow. We are never totally at peace; even in sleep we toss and turn, worrying and dreaming about all we have to do.

Anxiety is free-floating fear. Fear of forgetting something. Fear of remembering something. Fear of failure. Fear of success. Fear of not being able to sustain success.

We *are* attacked—by the insistent voice inside our own heads. We can secure our ground by saying to ourselves:

 **AFFIRMATION:**
I am not under siege.

See yourself as the Cat in the Hat, holding a cup and a cake, two books and the fish and a little toy ship and some milk and a dish—all of which you picked up with your own two hands.

—The Indispensable Woman

What a juggling act! Hopping from foot to foot, trying to keep from breaking anything.

Only a Seuss creation could manage it. Yet this is how we go through the day, frantically balancing more than the Cat in the Hat could hold.

Why don't we put something down?

❀ AFFIRMATION:
I only have two hands.

Anything you do not give freely and abundantly becomes lost to you. You open your safe and find ashes.
—Annie Dillard

We give so much, yet often it is sullied with anger and resentment.

We must give as true philanthropists, without measuring out the portions like misers.

The more we give, the more we have. When we open our arms to someone, their arms wrap back around us. When we generously share our thoughts and ideas, we become more excited, more inspired.

There is no need for martyrdom. Give freely, fearlessly, and from your heart.

❀ AFFIRMATION:
My safe sparkles with diamonds.

Live as if you liked yourself and it may happen.
                                        —*Marge Piercy*

Indispensable Women look to others to tell us we're good enough, smart enough, pretty enough.

Adopting a positive self-image—and believing it—makes us less dependent on what other people reflect back to us. Before long, we begin to believe—and expect—the very best of ourselves. We begin to live up to our highest expectations.

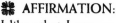 **AFFIRMATION:**
I like what I see.

Never let go of that fiery sadness called desire.
—Patti Smith

Sadness scares us. We don't want to feel the depth of our own yearning.

Yet that yearning speaks to us of what we need in order to be whole: meaningful work. Passionate embraces. Hours on the edge of the riverbank staring into the water.

When we flee from sadness into indispensability, we cut off the urgent voice of our desire. We lose the capacity to know what we want. And need. And deserve.

 **AFFIRMATION:**
I want so much.

*The great thing in this world is not so much where we are,
but in what direction we are moving.*

—*Anonymous*

A new person came into my household when my husband and I split up. I was lucky to find Suanne to help with the children, the housework, and provide back-up support.

Suanne represented a bridge between my old life and what was to come. At the time, when I looked at her, I was acutely aware of the loss and chaos in my life, feeling as if everything had suddenly gone to hell.

In retrospect, I see how well we weathered this transition. Life goes on.

 AFFIRMATION:
I am steadily moving ahead.

#4: *Let kids stay up late to make up for leaving town.*
— The Indispensable Woman

Acting out of guilt serves neither our children nor ourselves. We overcompensate for late business meetings by giving them sweets and letting them stay up past bedtime. In doing so we lose our precious little time for ourselves, and they just end up hitting the wall or waking up crabby the next morning.

Occasional treats are fine. But when they're meant to make up for lost time, they inevitably backfire.

❋ AFFIRMATION:
I will give my children what they need, not what makes them feel better.

> *I tried my best to please them, kept my bedroom neat,*
> *did my schoolwork well, brushed my hair a hundred*
> *strokes. . . .*
>
> —Joyce S. Petschek, The Silver Bird

We needed our parents literally in order to survive.
We did anything . . . *anything* we could to secure
their love.

The heartbreaking truth is that we are *still* trying.
Maybe not with our parents, but with friends, lovers,
employers—we do everything in our power to please.

Deep down we know that nothing will ever be
enough. But that doesn't stop us.

❁ AFFIRMATION:
If I never please them, I am still a superb human
being.

#7: *Clean the house before the cleaning lady comes.*
—*I.W. seminar*

We each have our own version: Folding the towels in hotel rooms. Triple-checking all nine hundred thousand words of my manuscript before it goes to the copy editor.

I know this is nuts. Yet our perfectionism drives us to present a flawless image, even to those we've specifically hired to deal with the flaws!

Letting other people see traces of our dirt is a sign of recovery. It means we're ready to stop pretending.

🍀 **AFFIRMATION:**
It's clean enough.

I was raised to sense what someone wanted me to be and be that kind of person. It took me a long time not to judge myself through someone else's eyes.

—*Sally Field*

Do you remember when Sally Field blurted out "You like me!" as she accepted her 1979 Oscar for *Norma Rae*?

Her outburst made me like her that much more. It also made me realize that no matter how high our star rises, we still crave approval from others in order to feel good about ourselves.

All our lives we strive to be what we think will merit applause. Even when *we're* satisfied with our performance, we seek external validation, whether we're wowing the masses or trying to get our mother to compliment us on a new haircut or promotion.

Bottom line is: no amount of approval is ever enough to convince us of our worth. Ultimately, we need to be able to say:

❀ AFFIRMATION:
I like me.

We teach what we need to learn.

—*Anonymous*

When I started presenting seminars, my mother said, "How can you tell other people what to do? You're the worst Indispensable Woman of all!"

"What do you think makes someone an expert?" I retorted.

We are always learning. That's what I like most about the concept of recovery: Success is marked by progress, not arrival. We needn't be "experts," just human beings learning and growing.

✽ AFFIRMATION:
I am my own best teacher.

I've been through it all, baby. I'm Mother Courage.
                                        —*Elizabeth Taylor*

Indispensable Women develop a thick skin in order to survive. Marching into battle is our modus operandi.

It's important to know we've got what it takes. Tenacity. The ability to get through the hard times with sheer guts and energy. We can muster our forces when needed.

But that doesn't mean we need to approach life with bayonets drawn. The trick is to stay tender even when we're tough.

❀ AFFIRMATION:
I have what it takes!

Little by little life returned to normal. The barbed wire which fenced us in did not cause us any real fear.

—*Elie Wiesel*

These words—from Holocaust survivor Elie Wiesel's description of a concentration camp—send chills down my spine.

To be able to consider life behind barbed wire as normal is tragic testimony to our incredible resiliency. We can handle, even transcend, the most terrifying realities with courage and hope.

Ultimately, each of us is imprisoned by our own terror. Think about the ways you fence yourself in with fear, real and imagined.

❀ AFFIRMATION:
I can move beyond my fear.

I had consented to give away my possessions one by one, as a kind of ransom for my own life, but by the time that I had nothing left, I myself was the lightest thing of all. . . .
—Isak Dinesen

We hold on tight . . . to our belongings, longings, and points of view.

There is no greater liberation than the lightness of letting go. Free and unfettered, indispensable in only the most sacred sense, we float through life without taking any hostages.

When we have nothing left, we have everything in the universe. We are free.

❀ AFFIRMATION:
I can give it all away.

I've been rich and I've been poor. Rich is better.
                                            —Sophie Tucker

I'm for spiritual materialism: the belief that we are all entitled to a life of abundance, including material comfort and security.

There's nothing wrong with making money. Money is time; it buys us the occasional night out or vacation we sorely need. It gives us the peace of mind to go to work with confidence that our children are well taken care of.

Our indispensability kicks in when we get hooked into making more and more money with less and less satisfaction. As long as financial success is the means to an end—not an end in itself—we're doing okay.

✿ AFFIRMATION:
Rich is better as long as wealth yields freedom.

A man who cares for his children is labeled Mr. Mom;
when men do their share of housework, they're applauded for
"helping."

—The Indispensable Woman

When Zoe was born, it infuriated me that people
would swoon whenever Gary was spotted feeding,
burping, or changing her (which he did often and
well). Needless to say, no one blinked when I did the
same things.

In the realm of child raising and domestic chores,
women are expected—and we expect ourselves—to
assume the lion's share.

As long as we perceive men as disabled or expendable in these areas, we won't get the help and support
we need. It's time to stop perpetuating the Mr. Mom
myth. Fathers are every bit as important and competent as mothers.

❇ AFFIRMATION:
I will do my best to support his role as Mr. Dad.

Nothing resembles pride so much as discouragement.
        —Mrs. Humphrey Ward, Amiel's Journal

As I struggled to understand this quotation *I* felt discouraged, then realized my sense of failure came from my stubborn pride in assuming I should quickly understand everything!

Indispensable Women are easily discouraged. When we miss the mark, we feel embarrassed and upset. Our natural response is to push harder in order to prove ourselves.

Pride gets in the way of personal progress. Discouragement isn't cause to rev up the motor. It's a gentle sign to slow down—we have something to learn.

❀ AFFIRMATION:
When I'm discouraged, I can relax, then try again.

For women to pump up their biceps or break into the club of hard-driving money grubbers on Wall Street is a peculiar and sad kind of liberation.

—*Alfie Kohn*

Years ago I was the only woman on an all-male sales force for a large radio station. At our Monday morning meetings we'd watch Vince Lombardi motivational films. Block 'em, knock 'em, and win, team, win!

Talk about being out in left field. They spoke a secret language of deception plays, handoffs, and passes. My sales technique consisted of making a personal connection, discovering what the customer wanted, and helping facilitate it.

As we've entered former male bastions, many women have bought into the Vince Lombardi school of success. It's not the only way. Or the best way.

AFFIRMATION:

I can be gentle, loving, and powerful in the world.

It is the time you have wasted for your rose that makes your rose so important.

—*Antoine de Saint-Exupery*

We're always coming and going. Every moment is meted out, accounted for, compartmentalized. We carry out our relationships on schedule and miss the simple pleasure of being together.

What we need is time to waste. Drawn-out dinners with dear friends. Lazy afternoons at the beach with sun-baked, sand-covered children.

When we have time to waste, we use it wisely—knowing and appreciating those we love.

AFFIRMATION:

It is the time I waste on them that makes things important.

Item: "Well, here's the new baby you told me you wanted. What do you have to say?" I asked my son Tony when Nicky, his brother, was born. "What I have to say," Tony said without a moment's hesitation, "is, I've changed my mind."

—Judith Viorst, Necessary Losses

Our indispensability is sometimes born of original competitiveness with our sisters and brothers. In our family of origin we learn the rules: what it takes to get Mother's love and Father's approval.

At my mother's sixty-fifth birthday party, my sister, Faith, made a toast. I panicked, then quickly composed a speech, determined to be more eloquent so as to assert my place in the family.

How nice it would be for family to feel like a sanctuary rather than a contest.

✳ **AFFIRMATION:**
I win when I stop competing.

What the people want is very simple. They want an America as good as its promise.

—*Barbara Jordan*

We've been described as a nation of adolescents in the throes of a perpetual identity crisis. We're desperate for answers, for miracle cures, for ways to perfect our self-image based on some elusive ideal.

Growing up, as individuals and as a nation, means releasing our egos from the endless search for perfection. If we appreciate who we are, what we have, and work on quietly improving the planet, we will have given much to the world.

❀ **AFFIRMATION:**
Why wait?

*At least Marge has figured out from these women's maga-
zines what shape face she has, Edie—somthing I'VE never
been sure of.*

—*Lynn (Jane Wagner)*

This line from Lily Tomlin's one-woman show, *The
Search for Signs of Intelligent Life in the Universe*, says so
much about women's endless battle to overcome our
conditioning and learn to accept and celebrate our
bodies.

This is no easy task. We scrutinize, criticize, even
self-mutilate in our insane drive to attain perfection.
We look in the mirror and see the imperfections—
cellulite, overbite, flabby arms, instead of seeing how
beautiful we are.

To be thankful is to praise God's work. This is how
we should behold ourselves—with glory and gratitude.

🎊 **AFFIRMATION:**
I am thankful for every square inch of my body.

Things that don't get better get worse.
                    —The Indispensable Woman

It is an illusion to put off recovery until later. Can change wait until we're *really* in trouble?

The fact is, the cost of indispensability creeps up slowly: the headache that doesn't let up, the marital tension that gets swept under the carpet, sloppy mistakes on the job.

Recovery is preventive medicine. Instead of waiting for the onset of a serious illness, let's begin our healing now.

❀ AFFIRMATION:
I don't have to collapse before I begin my recovery.

I must remember I am a helper. I can only be a catalyst for change.

—Rokelle Lerner

The addictive rush of coming to the rescue makes us lose sight of our human limitations. There is only so much any one human being can—or should—do for another.

Grandiosity must be kept in check, otherwise we delude ourselves into thinking we have the power to change other people.

Being a hero is powerfully seductive. Being a helper is profoundly satisfying.

❀ AFFIRMATION:
I can help other people make changes, but I cannot change them.

Continue to use your intuition—you can never solve a problem on the level at which it is born.

—*Lynn V. Andrews*

When we are stuck in our logical "left brain," we miss the truth, which is infinitely more subtle. In the search for the one-minute solution, we think too hard and move too fast: *Something's wrong! I'd better come up with a brilliant answer right away!*

To heal, we must go deeper. To a quieter place where we learn to trust our inherent wisdom and intuition. With patience and attention, the answers are revealed.

❀ AFFIRMATION:
I know exactly what to do.

The most exhausting thing in life is being insecure.
                    —*Anne Morrow Lindbergh*

The first time I went to a party as a "single" person,
post-divorce, I spent half my time in the bathroom
fiddling with my makeup and moussing my hair. The
rest of the time I nervously circulated, worrying about
how I looked and whether anyone liked me.

We are dragged down by the weight of our insecurity. It's like swimming against heavy waves; we sight
the shore but can only reach it with exhausting effort.

What would it be like to swim at even tide, with
steady, confident strokes, saying to ourselves:

❀ AFFIRMATION:
I will reach my destination.

I saw that nothing was permanent. You don't want to possess anything that is dear to you because you might lose it.

—Yoko Ono

Love is the greatest vulnerability of all. When we love fully and with abandon, we are raw, open to the possibility of great loss.

Believing that indispensability insures us against pain is the great illusion. There is no permanence, only the intense joy that comes of giving ourselves over to today. And tomorrow.

 **AFFIRMATION:**
Today is enough.

You've come a long way, baby!

—*Virginia Slims ad*

Ah, forbidden fruit! As a passionate ex-smoker, I was enthralled by those photographs of Victorian women hiding their cigarettes behind the folds of billowing white dresses.

Flash to the present: Now we can kill ourselves right out in the open! Hurrah!

Any way it's packaged, addiction is death. Recovery demands serious attention to life. To health. When we love ourselves enough to breathe cleanly, eat well, and exercise, we'll have come a long way.

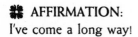 AFFIRMATION:
I've come a long way!

If love is the answer, could you please rephrase the question?

—*Lily Tomlin*

The mystery of love cannot be fathomed, only felt.

Still, we try. We sing the perfect song, dance the intricate steps we believe will make us finally and utterly indispensable in the eyes of our beloved.

What is lovable is invisible. Effortless. Beautifully beyond our control.

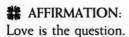 AFFIRMATION:
Love is the question.

Do you get so wrapped up in a project, you forget what else is happening around you?
                                    —The Indispensable Woman

Tunnel vision is a symptom of indispensability; we're so overly intent on the end goal, we can't tolerate any interruptions.

Learning to shift gears, to be more spontaneous and open to what's happening in the moment, means we're on the road to recovery. We welcome the unexpected, confident we can take a break, look around, and still stay on track.

 AFFIRMATION:
I can be focused without being fixated.

If only one could have two lives: the first in which to make one's mistakes . . . and the second in which to profit by them.

—D. H. Lawrence

We may have more lives than a cat, or perhaps this one is all there is. Many Eastern religions involve the idea of reincarnation—we keep coming back over many different lifetimes to work out our karma.

Whether we're here once or several times around, regret for our mistakes is a senseless waste of time and energy. What happened, happened. It had to happen in order for us to keep growing and evolving into more complete human beings.

Regret paralyzes. Self-forgiveness frees us to profit from our mistakes.

❀ AFFIRMATION:
I have no regrets.

The mother, poor invaded soul—finds even the bathroom door no bar to hammering little hands.

—*Charlotte Perkins Gilman*

When I lead Expecting Change workshops, there's always one "veteran mother" in the crowd with these encouraging words of wisdom: "Listen, once the baby's born, you'll be lucky to have time to go to the bathroom."

The truth is, children find us no matter where we are. My home has two thousand square feet. There are lots of places to play. So where are Zoe and Evan? Sitting on the floor of a tiny bathroom keeping me company, with or without an invitation.

Unless your newborn is screaming—and even then she can probably wait—you have the right to two minutes of privacy. And a locked door.

❀ AFFIRMATION:
I respect myself enough to say no to my children and anyone else who is stepping over my line.

*Money is only money, beans tonight and steak tomorrow.
So long as you look yourself in the eye.*

—*Meridel LeSueur*

Integrity matters above all else. No amount of worldly success or material security compares to the inner peace that comes from being able to look ourselves straight in the eye.

When we can meet our own gaze, we can make deeply authentic choices. Then the money will come. Or not. But we will be rich nonetheless.

 **AFFIRMATION:**
I can live on anything.

There are no ugly women, only lazy ones.
                              —*Helena Rubenstein*

We spend a small fortune in pursuit of beauty that only lies within, where makeup cannot reach. We apply a duskier shade of eye shadow, a softer blush to the imperfect contours of our God-given faces, so we'll finally feel pretty.

If I had a dollar for every lipstick relegated to the recesses of my bathroom drawer, I'd have a plane ticket to Miami. A lazy week off, letting the sun wash over my face, feeling the beauty that's real, that's mine.

 **AFFIRMATION:**
There are no ugly women, only insecure ones.

At times failure is very necessary for the artist. It reminds him that failure is not the ultimate disaster. And this reminder liberates him from the mean fussing of perfectionism.

—*John Berger*

Knowing we can fail and recover is the best antidote to defeat.

Failure is not only acceptable, it is a relief. We crawl, walk, falter, and finally find our way; in our stumbling we discover there is nothing to back away from except our own expectations of perfect balance.

The tightrope walker would be less riveting if he never swayed from side to side.

❀ AFFIRMATION:
There is a net.

#10: *Wake kids up to say good night so they can go to sleep.*

—*I.W. seminar*

That's how crazy it gets! In our misguided attempts to be the perfect wife, mother, friend, or employee, we confuse being needed with being necessary.

Who's it for? Do my children need that hug, or do I need to feel reassured of my place in their lives? Is it actually critical to stay late at work, or is it a way of inflating my importance in other people's eyes?

Honest appraisal prevents the arrogance of indispensability and the fear that feeds it.

❀ AFFIRMATION:
I am an integral part of the universe, not its center.

Creativity is the glory of being human.

—*John Bradshaw*

At our most indispensable, we are propelled by sheer will. *I have to, I must, I will die if I don't:* this is the driving force behind our behavior.

Creativity is the opposite of will. It is the glorious flow that writes the poem, rocks the child, is a healing force in the world.

When we calm down, breathe deeply, and let ourselves be, our creativity soars. We actually do more—and better—than when we try.

❀ AFFIRMATION:
I am naturally creative.

Nothing determines who we will become so much as those things we choose to ignore.

—*Sandor Minab*

We are focused on doing. On directing our energy and attention to accomplishing our goals.

But what we ignore—our health, relationships, spiritual hunger—equally defines who we become. The sin of omission, whether it's neglecting play, laughter, sleep, or long, leisurely lovemaking, is a sin against ourselves.

We have a choice: To be highly efficient machines. Or full, contented human beings.

❋ AFFIRMATION:
I will be aware of what I deny myself.

We can do anything we want as long as we stick to it long enough.

—Helen Keller

What a powerful role model of faith and persistence!

Certain things are worthy of such determination: following our calling, supporting a worthwhile cause, fighting for the love of our life.

When the stakes are high, the rewards truly worthwhile, then we can and should apply all our passion, guts, and drive. No holding back when we know what we want and want it with all our heart.

❧ AFFIRMATION:
I will harness my determination for my burning desires.

If you do not have a natural knack for dressing smartly, perhaps you should get some fabulous advice. There are many enlightened consultants around.

—Sondra Ray

From Sondra Ray, in the seventies, I learned that "I deserve love." Now I find out I deserve a fashion consultant so I can feel as good on the outside as the inside.

Makes perfect sense to me! Letting ourselves be loved and supported by enlightened consultants in every possible realm is a touchstone of recovery.

AFFIRMATION:
I am willing to be supported.

I base most of my fashion sense on what doesn't itch.
—*Gilda Radner*

Wouldn't it be great to be secure enough to care as much about comfort as vanity?

This is a worthwhile goal. To wear flannel when it's freezing, cotton in the blazing heat, and nothing itchy no matter what's gracing this month's *Cosmo* fashion spread.

Now *that's* smart dressing!

❋ AFFIRMATION:
I dress to feel great!

A sex symbol becomes a thing. I hate being a thing.
                                          —Marilyn Monroe

Personally I've always aspired to be a new sort of sex symbol. The *thinking* man's sex symbol.

It's okay—even great at times—to dress to the hilt, walk into a party knowing we look like a million bucks, with all eyes on us.

On the other hand, we must be careful not to objectify or degrade ourselves. We deserve love, no matter what we're wearing.

❧ AFFIRMATION:
I can be hot and sexy without compromising my integrity.

Always give yourself more time than you need.
                        —The Indispensable Woman

Indispensable Women race against the clock. Rushing in for a command performance just as the curtain rises makes us feel exhilarated and important.

It also stresses us out and annoys other people, especially when they're left staring at their watches.

Giving ourselves enough time—and being on time—is less dramatic but far more respectful. We walk into the room just like everyone else. No more. No less.

 AFFIRMATION:
I can give up the drama anytime.

It is misery, not pleasure, which contains the secret of the divine wisdom.

—Simone Weil

We can only truly empathize when we have plumbed the depths of our own pain.

There is no faking it. The humility born of wrenching pain tears open our hearts, sensitizing us to the suffering of others. Then we can go safely into the darkness, illuminating our journey and casting a light that leads the way.

 **AFFIRMATION:**
As I heal I become a healer.

Poverty is your treasure. Never exchange it for an easy life.

—*Zen saying*

At the height of my addiction, wealth was a carton of Marlboro Lights. Ten full packs warding off my terror of being without.

It would have been easier to keep smoking. Just as in many ways it's easier to die than to live.

But life proves infinitely richer. When we walk up a flight of stairs without gasping, when we wake in the morning and make a difficult choice, we are fully alive.

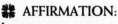 **AFFIRMATION:**
I am no prisoner.

> *You have got to own your days and live them, each one of them, every one of them, or else the years go right by and none of them belong to you.*
> —*Herb Gardner,* A Thousand Clowns

We hold our breath waiting for the perfect moment, the right person, the peak experience that makes life worthwhile.

Meanwhile we forget to breathe. To throw ourselves fully into every instant of every single day. The mundane as well as the magical.

Every experience—no matter how ordinary—makes us who we are and prepares us for who we are becoming. Every part of our lives has meaning; each moment must be claimed in full.

❊ AFFIRMATION:
Nothing is wasted.

I shall never believe that God plays dice with the world.
—Albert Einstein

We play our indispensability like a frantic board game: Up the ladder, down the chute, pass Go, take two love tokens, pray for doubles so we can roll again. . . .

But there is a bigger game plan, a cosmic strategy that goes way beyond our maneuverings. When we trust in a game plan that provides for our security and pleasure, we can throw the dice to the wind.

Wherever it lands, we are winners.

❄ AFFIRMATION:
All I have to do is play.

Existence is a strange bargain. Life owes us little; we owe it everything. The only true happiness comes from squandering ourselves for a purpose.

—William Cowper

What we owe life is what we owe ourselves: the right and responsibility to live with a deep sense of purpose. To pursue happiness on our own terms.

When we are passionately devoted to finding our most sacred place in the universe, indispensability has no meaning. We are focused, peaceful, in a state of confidence and grace.

 **AFFIRMATION:**
I believe I am here for a reason.

I can throw a fit; I'm a master at it.

—*Madonna*

We stomp our feet, pout, or pretend to be angrier than we are in order to be taken seriously. We throw a temper tantrum when two minutes' talking would do the trick.

We do this because we aren't convinced we deserve to get what we need. We make a ruckus because it's the only way we're sure we'll be heard.

This is false power. It doesn't serve us or further our ends. Simply and quietly asking for what we want is a more effective strategy.

 **AFFIRMATION:**
I can ask for what I want. And get it.

Imagine yourself on a desert island. Now take a temporary side-trip home and look at how everyone is managing without you. Are you really indispensable?

—The Indispensable Woman

No, not as indispensable as we think. Our children, our friends, even our jobs can survive without us for a few hours, a few days.

Of course we want to be needed, but not so much that it's impossible to tend to our own lives without feeling guilty or anxious.

Our guilt is grandiosity disguised. The truth is, no matter how great our contribution, life goes on with or without us.

❀ AFFIRMATION:
They'll live without me.

Trifles make perfection
And perfection is no trifle.

—*Michelangelo*

We get overwhelmed by the cosmic demands of perfection, when in fact, it is present in the smallest, most ordinary of encounters.

Sitting on a white plastic chair in front of the Kenwood Market, eating a blueberry muffin and watching six kids on bicycles on a summer's sidewalk parade.

It doesn't get any better.

❀ AFFIRMATION:
Perfection is everywhere when I pay attention.

Adopt the pace of nature,
her secret is patience.

—*Ralph Waldo Emerson*

Indispensable Woman Recovery Lesson: Slow down. *Way* down. Take a walk outside, a slow, quiet walk. Notice the treetops. Feel the sun, follow the clouds with your fingertip.

There is no rush. Only the shrill inner voice of our own obstinate creation.

Listen to the persistent voice. Listen to the soft breeze. Do you hear the contrast?

✿ AFFIRMATION:
Nature is my teacher.

The children are driven unconsciously in a direction that is intended to compensate for everything that was left unfulfilled in the lives of their parents.

—*Carl Gustav Jung*

We are "payback children," compelled by forces beyond our control, making ourselves indispensable to make up for our parents' stunted ambitions and lost dreams.

This is a dangerous legacy. We cannot fix their pain any more than they can prevent ours. The task is for each of us to live our own lives as best we can, without debt or apology, starting fresh as each human is meant to do.

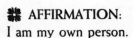 **AFFIRMATION:**
I am my own person.

> *By working faithfully eight hours a day, you may even-*
> *tually get to be a boss and work twelve hours a day.*
> —*Robert Frost*

When Kay—an accomplished Indispensable Woman —was promoted to vice president of a Fortune 500 company, she vowed to work harder than anyone ever had. And she expected her employees to follow suit.

After three weeks of staying until 11 P.M., her employees sent her this memo: "Please go home so we can."

There are situations in which a Herculean effort is called for: a sick child, Christmastime for retailers, the runners' marathon we've diligently trained for. Making a habit of overworking, on the other hand, is counterproductive. We burn out and set up other people to do the same.

✿ **AFFIRMATION:**
It's time to stop.

My idea of Superwoman is someone who scrubs her own floors.

—*Bette Midler*

Granted, Bette Midler's no domestic goddess, but then, *she* can probably afford help.

Most of us do have to scrub our own floors, and that's on top of everything else we do.

What constitutes "Superwoman" varies, but with few exceptions we've been socialized to expect ourselves to take on the bulk of household chores. I, for one, grew up in a family with a kitchen floor clean enough to eat off of. No matter how hard I try, *my* kitchen floor would still do better with a tablecloth.

Maybe it's time to stop trying.

 **AFFIRMATION:**
Superwoman is dead.

Until sexism is wiped out, women will continue to feel they must protect their security by making themselves indispensable.

—The Indispensable Woman

As long as we are expected to be the primary caregivers, as long as we make seventy-two cents to a man's dollar, our dependency upon men continues. We feel compelled to bend over backwards, to not make waves in order to remain in their favor.

This is a costly compromise. The honest intimacy possible between women and men is diminished by this dubious contract.

We will all benefit when equality reigns; when we are together, not out of dependence, but rather out of mutual desire.

❄ AFFIRMATION:
I will hold out for equality.

How sick one gets of being "good," how much I should respect myself if I could burst out and make everyone wretched for twenty-four hours.

—Alice James

"Sugar and spice and everything nice." *Please!*

The little girl within gets tired of being good. Always on guard, anticipating everyone's wishes and desires. What a relief to let down and be ourselves!

For the next twenty-four hours, make a point of *not* doing anything with the express purpose of gaining approval or affection. Be aware of how it feels to express all parts of yourself, the wretched as well as the wonderful. Notice what being real does to your self-respect.

 AFFIRMATION:
I don't have to be good all the time.

A woman will always sacrifice herself if you give her the opportunity. It's her favorite form of self-indulgence.
                                        —W. Somerset Maugham

When we give in order to massage our egos and magnify our self-importance, we end up giving little of value. The right reason for sacrifice comes from feeling moved, loving, and inspired. Then generosity becomes a form of gratitude.

The difference can be felt. Indispensability glorifies the self. Sacrifice is selfless.

✿ AFFIRMATION:
Today I am grateful to give to other people for no other reason than that it gives me pleasure.

For fast-acting relief try slowing down.

—*Lily Tomlin*

To reduce stress, we can stuff down antacids or slow down our lifestyle. The first is fast-acting; the second long-lasting.

As long as we merely treat symptoms, we can't make real headway on recovering our health and well-being. Chronic anxiety manifested by stomachaches and headaches tells us that our indispensability is eating us alive.

Over-the-counter remedies merely medicate the problem. Making changes in our lives gets to the root of it.

❀ AFFIRMATION:
If I attend to the cause, the cure will take care of itself.

I'm living so far beyond my income that we may be said to be living apart.

—*e. e. cummings*

We pursue wealth, thinking the more we have, the more we're worth. Sometimes we get in trouble. Overdrawn. Over our limit. Over our head.

It's just not worth it. In this endless cycle of consumerism and debt we trap ourselves into having to produce more and more just to keep from sinking into quicksand.

The more we spend, the harder it is to find a foothold. The first solid step is closing the gap between earning and spending. Paying for a lifestyle that's killing us—no matter how capable we are of supporting it—is too high a price to pay.

❈ AFFIRMATION:
I have enough.

For people who like peace and quiet, a phoneless cord.
                                        —*Anonymous*

The first time my husband and I took our children to McGuire's Piney Ridge Lodge, they instantly blissed out. I attributed their happiness to the lakefront cottage, daily pony rides, and chocolate pudding on the American-plan buffet.

No way. They were ecstatic over what was missing: *the phone!* No jangling in the middle of dinner. No business calls to compete with them for Mom and Dad's attention.

I think about this as I drive on the freeway watching businessmen weave in and out of traffic, cradling their cordless phones. How did we ever live without this incredible invention? How much peace and quiet are we denying ourselves by keeping the lines perpetually open?

❈ **AFFIRMATION:**
They'll call back.

If you always do what interests you, at least one person is pleased.

—*Katharine Hepburn's mother*

Indispensability is a losing proposition. In trying to please everyone else, we please no one.

We will never be on everyone's hit parade! We won't even begin to endear ourselves to most people, because they have their own agendas, which we can't possibly fulfill.

We do better to go about our lives with purpose, focusing on what interests, stimulates, and pleases us. Then, at least, we can say, "For better or for worse, I am my own person."

❀ AFFIRMATION:
I would rather inspire respect than gain approval.

Like waves incessantly pounding the shore, a sense of urgency propels us.

—The Indispensable Woman

Urgency and drama drive us in our effort to meet our goals. Ironically, the more frantic we become, the less artful and effective we are in achieving those goals. Our breathing is labored, our judgment lessened when we feel anxious and overwhelmed.

Success comes when we peacefully ride the waves, when we calmly approach each task with the confidence that we will reach the shore.

❊ **AFFIRMATION:**
What I do is important. What I feel about it is urgent.

The moment of change is the only poem.

—*Adrienne Rich*

In Minneapolis, where I live, Halloween marks the change of season. Summer is over; the crisp autumn air holds the promise of winter to come.

As the leaves turn and fall, so do we change. With each season of our lives, we have less need for artifice. Less need to don new masks, acquire fresh identities to define who we are becoming.

As fall turns to winter, we prepare to stay warm, to become more comfortable in our own changing skin.

❄ AFFIRMATION:
I am myself, through each season, always.

I finally figured out the only reason to be alive is to en-joy it.

—Rita Mae Brown

It may not be the *only* reason, but it's right up there near the top of the list!

Life is more than work. Being alive—truly alive—means savoring the opportunities for pleasure and joy that present themselves at every turn.

Yet we live as if happiness were a side benefit, the reward we get for working ourselves to the bone.

No! Pleasure comes naturally in the process of putting our energy where our heart is. Meaningful work is enjoyable in and of itself. Intimate relationships based on true commitment are pleasurable even when difficult and challenging.

If we're not enjoying ourselves, it's time to reassess how we're living.

❊ AFFIRMATION:
I have one life.

> *Men are taught to apologize for their weaknesses, women*
> *for their strength.*
>
> —*Lois Wyse*

If this statement is true—and I believe it is—then it is
equally true that men are taught to celebrate their
strength and women their weaknesses.

All of us are hurt by this sort of sexist conditioning.
Men deprived of their right to be vulnerable cannot
possibly grow. Women denied power and strength
become indispensable as a way to gain a sense of
control over their lives.

We must all claim our strength and weakness, without overcompensating on either side.

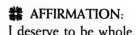

AFFIRMATION:
I deserve to be whole.

Standing here in front of the mirror, I wonder if I am at a philosophical intersection where vanity, vogue, fear of aging and insecurity meet and collide.

—Mary-Lou Weisman

Aging gracefully is a lovely notion—until age catches up with us. Then we struggle with self-love versus self-loathing, the latter made almost inevitable by a culture obsessed with youth: Twenty is sexier than thirty; after forty, forget it.

Entering mid-life, we wince at our reflection in the mirror, wishing for a tauter, wrinkle-free countenance. We spend good money on cosmetic concoctions promising to ward off the marks of age. We contemplate plastic surgery, the ultimate negation of time.

The only victory is in coming to accept ourselves as we ripen and mature. To see the lines in our faces as the map of our lives.

❈ AFFIRMATION:
I keep getting better.

Happiness is not something you experience, it's something you remember.

—Oscar Levant

The pursuit of pleasure prevents its full experience in the moment. We hang our cameras around our necks like tourists, worried about arranging the perfect pose against the most scenic background. We get great photos for our vacation scrapbook.

Meanwhile the sights, sounds, and subtleties of new, exotic experiences pass us right by. Sunset on the beach is a potential pretty postcard rather than a glorious instant when time stops. The flavor of a foreign culture—whether it's Pittsburgh or Paris—is one step removed as we try to capture it for posterity.

Memories are nice, but not at the price of immediacy. Souvenirs pale next to priceless moments in the here and now.

❊ AFFIRMATION:
It's happening right now.

#8: Make a list of everything I have to do so I know exactly what to worry about.

—*I.W. seminar*

Why do we keep making lists? What demons are held at bay by our relentless jottings—the futile attempt to bring order to our lives?

Organization is an illusion. We fool ourselves, thinking that if we put it all down, number it, we can get a handle on the myriad demands that dominate our thoughts. But the relief is fleeting. If anything, we create more tension by confronting the written roster of our indispensability. The longer the list, the more inclined we are to fast-forward, worrying about what's left to do.

Perhaps it's time to toss the lists and, instead, choose one thing to do, do it, and then calmly go on to the next.

❈ AFFIRMATION:
Today I will resist making lists.

To have courage for whatever comes in life—everything lies in that.

—*Saint Teresa of Avila*

Life is bursting with surprises, a reality Indispensable Women stubbornly resist.

We like knowing what's going to happen next. We plan, commit to the plan, execute the plan, and then, *boom*, life intervenes and we are forced to react spontaneously in the moment.

How we fare in the face of unpredictability says a lot about us. Are we rigid, unable to meet contingencies? Or can we summon the courage and self-trust to deal with what comes?

Often what comes is better than anything we could have planned. Being open is its own reward.

❀ AFFIRMATION:
I couldn't have planned it better myself.

The only time a woman really succeeds in changing a man is when he's a baby.

—Natalie Wood

Almost from the moment we meet, we try to change our mates—get them to be more involved, more communicative, more intimate in the way they express their emotions.

This is a waste of time. As long as we hold to the belief that we can manipulate change, we will be frustrated and disappointed. Compromise? Certainly. Make him into someone he's not? A project doomed to failure.

❈ AFFIRMATION:
I will accept and love him. I cannot change him.

I believe that what woman resents is not so much giving herself in pieces as giving herself purposelessly.
                                    —*Anne Morrow Lindbergh*

It is a testimony to our talent that we can shift gears so easily. One minute we're making Rice Krispies bars for the block party, soon we're doling out heartfelt advice to a friend, next we're running a meeting with savvy and skill.

At times we feel fragmented and overwhelmed by the rapid pace of our constant identity changes. What saves us is the conviction we feel for what we are doing. When each choice is intentional and clear, the pieces come together.

❊ AFFIRMATION:
I am purposefully choosing to give in many places.

> *One never notices what has been done; one can only see what remains to be done.*
>
> —Marie Curie

Perhaps that's the key to great discovery—concentrating on what lies ahead instead of dwelling on past accomplishments.

But a balance is necessary. Success depends in part on our capacity to appreciate achievements, to integrate and use what we've learned along the way.

When we're too focused on conquering the next big challenge, we cheat ourselves of the deep sense of reward that's rightfully ours. It's worthwhile to stop, at least for a moment, take in what we've done, and feel really good about it.

❈ AFFIRMATION:
I have done a lot. There's still a lot to do.

Always aim for achievement and forget about success.
—Helen Hayes

Years ago I attended a parent/child preschool program. One morning a specialist in early childhood education talked to us about giving positive feedback to our children. She said, "When your child paints a picture, don't say: 'What a great picture! I'm so proud of you for painting it!' Instead, say, 'Wow! You really worked hard getting all that green and purple paint on the paper!' "

I understood the difference. The first statement conveys approval for the end product of our child's performance; the second communicates appreciation of the effort.

I try to remember this distinction when I get caught up with product instead of process.

❧ AFFIRMATION:
Success is in the doing.

I am a kind of paranoic in reverse; I suspect people of trying to make me happy.

—J. D. Salinger

Indispensable Women are justifiably suspicious of how other people perceive us. We've done such a good job of selling ourselves, we're never sure if we're liked for our real selves or because of a masterful marketing job.

The only way to find out is to remove the packaging and let other people see what's inside. If we're being genuine, we have nothing to fear, no risk of being found out.

Our paranoia is lessened when we feel confident that others are attracted to us for the right reasons—because of who we really are. Then, instead of mistrusting affection and attention, we can bask in it.

❋ AFFIRMATION:
There are many genuine reasons why people like me.

If it weren't for the last minute, nothing would get done.
—*Anonymous*

In our perfectionism we procrastinate, waiting until we're down to the wire, paralyzed by fear that our best effort won't be good enough.

Rushing only increases our anxiety. What we create at the last minute is colored by stress and adrenaline; the most we can hope for is relief rather than the calm pleasure that comes from a job well done.

Better we should move slowly and carefully. Then, instead of a final mad rush for the finish line, we can stop and take time to appreciate our work.

❋ AFFIRMATION:
The last minute isn't the best time to start.

Love must not entreat or demand. Love must have the power to find its own way to certainty.

—*Hermann Hesse*

Today is the birthday of someone very special to me. He is forty-one.

With this amazing man I am learning to love and be loved. Not because I have impressed him or won him over, but because of the little, indefinable qualities that make up one's essence: funny gestures, endearing mannerisms, dirt under my fingernails that he claims to adore at least as much as my artfully calculated wardrobe.

I am learning to be with him without making myself indispensable, without fear of asking for what I want, without second-guessing his every desire or trying to circumvent his pain.

Together we are learning to trust in a deep, abiding connection. Together we are learning to follow what is real and certain.

❈ AFFIRMATION:
I will allow love to find its own way.

If you can't help it, don't think about it.

—*Carmel Myers*

Now there's sound advice! What's the point of making ourselves crazy when there's nothing we can do?

Yet turning off the motor of our anxiety is easier said than done. It runs against our grain; even when we know better, we obsessively worry and fret.

Our eight-year-old forgets to take her science project to school and we spin our wheels worrying over whether to bring it to her or let her face the consequences. Our routine blood test results are two days late and we can't stop imagining the worst.

What we *can* help is worth thinking and doing something about. What we *can't* help is best let go of. Surrender makes it possible to stop worrying about what's beyond our control.

❀ AFFIRMATION:
I will act when I can make a difference.

Live in day-tight compartments.

—*Dale Carnegie*

We stress ourselves out worrying about tomorrow and the next day and the next. Breaking our responsibilities into day-tight compartments makes life considerably more manageable.

Today is Tuesday. I need to water my plants, fold the laundry, and clean the top of my desk. Tomorrow is Wednesday. If my desk is clean, I can pay the bills; on Thursday I won't have to concern myself with any of this and can turn my attention to something else.

One day at a time: the all-time best recovery advice. It applies equally to abstinence from chemical dependency, overeating, gambling, and indispensability, or to any other courageous effort we make to improve the quality of our lives.

❈ AFFIRMATION:
All I have to do today is what I have to do today.

Mistakes are part of the dues one pays for a full life.
—Sophia Loren

We think if we make ourselves indispensable enough, we will either avoid making mistakes altogether or be so good that they'll be overlooked or forgiven. But mistakes are how we learn, how we grow, the inevitable result of throwing ourselves fully into the fray of life.

The only way to avoid making mistakes is to lock ourselves in a room and never come out. And then just think of all we'd miss!

❋ AFFIRMATION:
Mistakes are part of the deal.

We challenge one another to be funnier and smarter. . . .
It's the way friends make love to one another.
                                          —*Annie Gottlieb*

Just as the most passionate lovers need to get out of bed sometimes, we need to be able to "turn it off" with our friends.

One man I know complains that he doesn't like going to parties anymore because his friends constantly egg him on to "tell the one about . . ." He feels pushed into the spotlight, when sometimes he'd rather blend into the background.

Pressure has no place in friendship. If we're feeling smart or funny, fine. If we're sad, shy, or quiet, also fine.

❋ AFFIRMATION:
I can relax with my friends.

It seems to me I spent my life in car pools, but you know, that's how I kept track of what was going on.

—*Barbara Bush*

That's where the real stuff happens: sitting on the front stoop licking Popsicles . . . schlepping kids to softball practice. Although we look forward to the "big events"—piano recitals and prom dates—it's the unstructured, relaxed time we spend with our children that holds the most value.

These days Barbara Bush spends her hours in motorcades; I understand her nostalgia for simpler times, just hanging out with her kids, when she was only first lady to her family.

It makes me glad it's my turn to drive the car pool.

❧ AFFIRMATION:
An ordinary life is a full one.

The Expert has the right answer, the perfect solution, and the best way to handle everything.
                                        —The Indispensable Woman

We build up our work load by cultivating a reputation as The Expert. Even when we doubt ourselves, we act as if we were right on top of a situation.

This is a great way to exhaust our energies—by continually pretending to have it all together.

Being The Expert also alienates us from the significant people in our lives; we rob others of the opportunity to give valuable input and feel good about themselves.

Everyone benefits when we take turns being The Expert.

❈ AFFIRMATION:
I don't have to be The Expert in order to be liked and respected.

Don't be humble; you're not that great!

—Golda Meir

Humility and grandiosity are opposite sides of the same coin. Too good or not good enough are both ways of separating ourselves from the rest of the human race. Both are self-destructive; both come from our reluctance to accept that we are perfectly ordinary human beings just like everyone else—sometimes insecure, other times grand and heroic.

False humility is a sign that we are falling into indispensability, that we need to inflate ourselves by making a big deal of either our accomplishments or our shortcomings.

The truth is, we are fine. There's no need to shout it from the rooftops, but there's no need to whisper either.

AFFIRMATION:

I get to feel good about myself.

The thing women have to learn is that no one gives you power. You just take it.

—Roseanne Arnold

And, I'd add: no one can take it away, either.

This is a hard lesson for women to learn. We have been taught to feel powerful through others—by virtue of being nice, compliant, doing what we think other people want. As long as our parents, lovers, friends, employers, even children think highly of us, we experience a temporary surge of self-worth.

Real power comes from deep knowledge of ourselves and an inner belief in our inherent value, aside from anything we say or do. Real power isn't acquired; it's our natural legacy in the world.

❦ AFFIRMATION:
I accept my power.

Somebody should tell us, right at the start of our lives, that we are dying. Then we might live life to the limit, every minute of every day.

—Michael Landon

These words, spoken by the actor Michael Landon a month before his death from cancer, seem apt for the anniversary of President John F. Kennedy's death.

Time stopped on that historic day in Dallas; an entire nation watched in horror as Camelot was destroyed. In the aftermath of the assassin's bullet, we are vividly reminded that each moment of every day is precious.

Let us live life to the fullest, for we never know what tomorrow will bring.

✿ AFFIRMATION:
My mortality inspires me to live life to the limit.

Never mistake motion for action.

—*Ernest Hemingway*

What a perfect distinction for Indispensable Women, always on the move, but not necessarily headed in any meaningful direction.

It's easy to confuse constant motion with purposeful activity, especially when we're on the treadmill. We fool ourselves into thinking we're getting somewhere, when we're really just running in place.

Constant motion is a symptom of indispensability. Action is a sign of recovery. Here's how to tell the difference: The first is ragged and compulsive; the second is calm and intentional.

❀ AFFIRMATION:
I will move with a purpose.

Keep your face to the sunshine and you cannot see the shadows.

—*Helen Keller*

Helen Keller's triumph of spirit against enormous odds inspires us all.

She reminds us that the shadows of our fear can be overcome if we are willing. Thinking about the dual challenges of deafness and blindness makes us appreciate all we have—our senses, our health, the miracle of being able to see the light and feel the sunshine on our face.

For all that we worry about—and we worry a lot!—we have so much. It's important to remember that.

❀ AFFIRMATION:
I am grateful.

First and finally, we lose connection with ourselves. We haven't the time or peace to tap our deepest recesses, the part of us that feels holy and connected to God.
                                    —The Indispensable Woman

Holidays can be exhausting marathons of cooking, entertaining, and the roller coaster of family dynamics.

This year, make Thanksgiving a real holiday—a holy day. A day in which you put aside time to take stock of your life. Reflect on the choices you have made, the people you love, whether you are fulfilling your purpose and destiny. Take time to reconnect with yourself, with nature, with your own sense of what's holy and sacred in the universe.

Mark Thanksgiving with renewed commitment to live a life you can be thankful for.

❀ AFFIRMATION:
Thank you.

Where do you go to get anorexia?

—*Shelley Winters*

At the risk of seeming irreverent, I chose this quote because it captures how we feel when we gorge ourselves.

It is our fear of scarcity—that there won't be enough, whether it's turkey or love—that makes us stuff ourselves to the gills. We eat way beyond the comfort point instead of stopping when we're full.

This year, let's leave room to be conscious of the true spirit of Thanksgiving: as a time to be aware of those who are less fortunate and express our gratitude for the abundance in our lives.

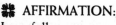 **AFFIRMATION:**
I am full.

Cleaning your house while your kids are still growing
Is like shoveling the walk before it stops snowing.
                    —*Phyllis Diller*, Household Hints

We endlessly pick up and put away the Magic Markers, unmatched socks, and fragments of toys. Ten minutes later, the room looks as if a cyclone had hit.

Why bother? Because of the pleasure and pride we take in creating an orderly home with a minimum of disarray.

Housework is a great lesson in letting go. We need to focus on how good we feel when our home is sparkling, rather than being frustrated by how quickly our handiwork is undone. If we can glean satisfaction moment to moment, room to room, we can enjoy the fruits of our labor, no matter how short-lived.

✻ **AFFIRMATION:**
I clean my house because I like my house clean.

We are so vain that we even care for the opinion of those we don't care for.

—*Marie Ebner von Eschenbach*

My friends tease me about changing clothes three times before taking out the garbage! But who knows what could be waiting for me when I open that door?

Why do we need the whole world's approval? What deep insecurity makes us care so much about what everybody thinks?

If we think highly of ourselves, then we can put criticism *or* compliments in the right perspective.

�֎ AFFIRMATION:
Who cares?

The two hardest things to handle in life are failure and success.

—*Unknown*

In the loop of indispensability, failure makes us feel pressured to succeed, and success makes us fearful of failure.

Neither contributes to the confidence we need in order to be our best, whether in work or in love.

Performance fears make us tight and anxious; nothing flows when we're caught up in proving ourselves. Success comes naturally when we relax and enjoy what we're doing, being attentive without worrying about taking first place—or last.

❈ AFFIRMATION:
There is no such thing as failure, as long as I'm being my best.

The way I see it, if you want the rainbow, you gotta put up with the rain.

—Dolly Parton

Last night, driving home, I saw a double rainbow that followed a downpour so intense I had to pull off the road.

The sky went from gray to black to azure in a matter of minutes. The contrast was stunning; the streaks of rainbow stretched into the distance as I sat marveling at how the darkest storm clouds are transformed into the most breathtaking beauty.

So it is that the most difficult times are followed by a deeper appreciation of life's hues. We can't have one without the other; rain and rainbows—pain and joy to balance one another.

AFFIRMATION:
Bring on the rain.

Imagination is the highest kite one can fly.
                                    —*Lauren Bacall*

Anything we dream becomes a possibility.

That is why it's so important to let our imagination fly. Indispensable Women are full of energy and ambition, yet too often we limit our horizons by a rigid definition of self.

When we cling to an absolute identity—I know who I am, and I'm not about to change!—we stunt our own growth.

It's great to have a firm idea of who we are. It's even better to ride the wild winds of who we are becoming.

✿ AFFIRMATION:
I give myself the freedom to fly.

If truth is beauty, how come no one has their hair done in a library?

—Lily Tomlin

If beauty is truth, how come no one reads great literature at the beauty shop?

Because we'd rather flip through *Vogue* while having our hair colored and brows waxed. Not to mention making small talk with other women under the dryers!

It's relaxing and replenishing to take a break from the rigorous demands of our lives. We put ourselves in expert hands and walk out feeling beautiful and ready to go back to work.

❄ AFFIRMATION:
The truth is, it's important to feel beautiful.

> *Big doesn't necessarily mean better. Sunflowers aren't better than violets.*
>
> —Edna Ferber

Travelers from all over the world visit Byerly's, Minneapolis's 24-hour, 93,000-square-foot shopping extravaganza complete with live-lobster tank, gourmet candy store, and a one-of-a-kind gift gallery featuring high-priced crystal, porcelain, and even a precious Lalique table from France.

Going to Byerly's is an event; it's the place to see and be seen.

But personally, I prefer Ralph and Jerry's on University and Fourth. Handmade signs, dust in the aisles, and the same hippies who've been hanging out for twenty years. Less intimidating, more intimate, and for my money, a sweeter place to be.

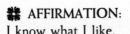 **AFFIRMATION:**
I know what I like.

The first wealth is health.

—Ralph Waldo Emerson

It's tempting to overlook our health amid the dizzying demands of our packed schedules. We grab a donut and coffee instead of making ourselves a healthy lunch. We postpone our annual checkup instead of making it a priority.

But health should be the priority! Without it everything else is lost. We can't accomplish our goals when we're dragging ourselves around sick and drained of energy.

It's never too late to start taking our well-being seriously. Make a commitment to do one thing, now, to improve the quality of your life.

✿ AFFIRMATION:
I'm worth it.

Sooner or later I'm going to die, but I'm not going to retire.
—*Margaret Mead*

Aging doesn't mean we close up shop; we merely cut back our hours.

For Indispensable Women the thought of retirement is deadly. What will I do if I'm not working? Who *am* I if I'm not *doing* something?

There are so many wonderful things to do, and they all have value. Tending a garden. Spending time with children or grandchildren. Reading a book that takes more than three hours to finish.

I, for one, can't wait!

 **AFFIRMATION:**
There are many stages of life.

As I become intimate with my children's flaws and imperfections, I rediscover my own.
                                    —The Indispensable Woman

Today, on Zoe's birthday, I realize again that having children is at once elevating and humbling. We marvel at being given these wondrous creatures; yet we inevitably face their—and our own—imperfections. We are continually challenged to love our children despite their flaws. And each time we fail *them*, we face our own fallibility, ideally with courage and the willingness to change.

As we unconditionally accept our children, heaping on love and encouragement after their mistakes, we heal our own remnants of shame. We learn life's important lesson: We are all imperfect. This makes us no less worthy of love.

❄ AFFIRMATION:
Loving my children is an opportunity to learn to love myself.

One of my problems is that I internalize everything. I can't express anger. I grow a tumor instead.

—*Woody Allen*

Anger terrifies Indispensable Women. We either stuff it or overamplify instead of directly expressing our feelings.

Deep down we don't believe we have the right to be angry. We're terrified that showing it will make other people stop loving us; instead we turn anger inward, where it ferments into self-loathing and shame.

Breaking this malignant cycle requires the courage to say:

AFFIRMATION:

I'm angry. This is why. This is what I want.

I can't believe I forgot to have children.

—*Popular saying*

I've seen this saying on T-shirts, bumper stickers, and in various cartoons. I'm always struck by its bittersweet humor—a poignant statement of contemporary women's struggle between the longing for motherhood and career.

Every choice is equally worthy of respect. What matters is that we act out of a conscious consideration of what we want—in our heart of hearts—not only now, but in the long run.

May our lives never be so full that we forget to think about what will fulfill us.

❈ AFFIRMATION:
I'm not forgetting any of the important things.

> *Both artist and lover know that perfectionism is not lovable. It is the clumsiness of a fault that makes a person lovable.*
>
> —Joseph Campbell

It is the idiosyncratic, sweet stumbling that endears others to us. Yet we place a great demand on ourselves to present a perfect front in place of our similarly flawed selves.

Here's an experiment: The next time you're tired, crabby, and in a bad mood, call up a friend. Groan and whine and be just as miserable as you feel. Bet you anything (unless you do this regularly) you'll get back love and encouragement—partly because misery loves company, mostly because other people love us when we let down our guard.

�֎ AFFIRMATION:
I will let other people see me as I am.

As our hands held before our eyes hide the tallest mountain, so the routine of everyday life keeps us from seeing the vast radiance and the secret wonders that fill our world.

—Chasidism, eighteenth century

We become immersed in our indispensability, blinded by endless activities and distractions.

But every moment presents a choice: We can close tight our eyes and shutter the light. Or we can throw open the windows to the wonders that surround us.

Each time we notice the kitchen curtains dancing in the breeze, each time we get down on our knees and see straight into our children's eyes, we are more alive, more aware of the beauty in the world. We look up and glimpse the top of the mountain.

❀ **AFFIRMATION:**
Today I remove my hands from before my eyes in order to see the world in its entirety.

The only reason I would take up jogging is so that I could hear heavy breathing again.

—*Erma Bombeck*

I know this quote is about sex—or the lack of it—but first, let's talk about exercise.

The two are connected. Indispensable Women tend to be either sedentary workaholics (eighty hours on the job) or workout fanatics. Neither is conducive to love or romance; both are ways of sublimating our need for sex.

Both exercise and lovemaking are important to revitalize our sensuality and bring balance to our lives. We need the glow and exhilaration that come from working up a sweat.

🏵 **AFFIRMATION:**
Sex is great exercise. Exercise is great for sex.

Boyfriends weren't friends at all, they were prizes, escorts, symbols of achievement.

—*Susan Allen Toth*

For those of us who came of age in the fifties and sixties, getting a boy was the ultimate coup.

Our status soared when we boasted about a prom date or sported an I.D. bracelet. We were the envy of our friends!

Male attention still feels good, but we don't need to go steady to feel like a success. As we come into our own, we no longer need to collect men—using them as Intimacy Objects or Attention Getters—in order to enhance our own image in the world.

❄ AFFIRMATION:
I don't need reflected glory. My glory comes from within.

Behind the Indispensable Woman's facade is a desperate need for security.

—The Indispensable Woman

We wish other people could see beneath our facade; we want them to know—without telling them—that we are vulnerable, in need of acknowledgment and affection.

Yet everything about us screams independence! Under control! Doing just fine without any help from anyone, thank you very much!

We need to feel loved, needed, necessary, secure. That doesn't make us less competent, merely more approachable.

It is up to us to make sure the inside matches the outside. It is up to us to stop giving double messages, so we can get what we need.

AFFIRMATION:
My facade hides the real me and keeps me from getting what I need.

Give me a dozen such heartbreaks, if that would help me to lose a couple of pounds.

—Colette

God, the lengths we'll go to in order to attain some magazine's ideal of perfection! In college, I knew girls who had sex constantly because they'd heard it was a good way to burn up calories!

We grow up, lose and gain hundreds of pounds, and continue to make ourselves crazy over the stomach that sticks out, the thighs that meet in the middle.

Twenty years out of college, many of us are on the "Divorce Diet"—a major heartbreak, a lot of suffering, and look at me—finally a size 8!

❋ AFFIRMATION:
There must be an easier way.

> *You don't get ulcers from what you eat. You get ulcers*
> *from what's eating you.*
>
> —*Vicki Baum*

We can only ignore what eats away at us for so long, without paying for it in the form of physical illness.

If we cover our feelings with indispensability and let them fester, pain pops up all over the place. We get headaches, stomachaches, toothaches, backaches. I know a woman who in one year was tested for Lyme disease, chronic fatigue syndrome, mononucleosis, and AIDS. When she finally faced that she wasn't getting what she needed in her marriage—and got out—the symptoms cleared up.

We must sit still and listen to what our bodies are telling us!

✿ **AFFIRMATION:**
Getting sick is my body's way of saying "Stop and listen to me! There's a lot going on inside!"

I am what I am. Take it or leave me.

—Rosario Morales

It's great to be self-confident enough to say this and mean it. Still, I wonder whether we need be quite so strident to get our point across.

As we begin to recover from indispensability, we may be overzealous in setting boundaries and asserting our independence. We've acquiesced so long, it's natural to go a little overboard.

Gradually the pendulum swings back toward center. We don't take any grief from anyone, but we're gentler in our approach.

❀ AFFIRMATION:
I am what I am. Take it or tell me how you feel about it.

I have worn myself out trying to find a man who lived up to my idealistic notions.

—Hirbayashi Taiko

We start out projecting our needs onto our mates; little by little we come to realize that he is who he is, not who we'd like him to be.

In the process we become disillusioned. When we have to face reality, we either try to change him or search for someone who more closely matches our fantasy.

This is an exhausting and endless quest. What we are looking for cannot be found in another person; real love does not occur upon meeting the "perfect mate." It requires stripping away the illusion that any one person can provide the deep peace and security we're constantly seeking.

✤ AFFIRMATION:
When I stop looking, I can see what's really there.

We are slaves to the cost of living.

—*Carolina Maria de Jesus*

The more we have, the more we want. Clothes, cars, CD players, there's no end to our consumerism once we get rolling.

The pattern is self-defeating: We put ourselves in debt in order to keep buying the toys and treats we need to reward ourselves for how hard we have to work. Instead of reevaluating our values, we are trapped by a lifestyle that costs way too much.

Many of us are caught in this vicious cycle. The way out is to take stock of what we have, what we need, and whether we're in over our head. If so, it's time to get back to basics.

✿ AFFIRMATION:
I want a lot. But I need little.

I never said, "I want to be alone." I only said, "I want to be left alone."

—Greta Garbo

Garbo—enigmatic to the end—protected her privacy to the day she died.

Did she end up isolated and alone? How many of us, fiercely guarding our independence, not wanting to be told *how* to live—live our lives without friendship and companionship?

What can we learn from this? When we assert our independence, set boundaries, or close ourselves to input and support—we must be sure to not push other people away. We must tell other people—straight out —that we want them in our lives.

❇ **AFFIRMATION:**
I don't have to be lonely.

When you stop making yourself indispensable, you get more done.

—The Indispensable Woman

Why? Because you can think straight!

When we're running around crazily, we can hardly concentrate, much less do a quality job. We rush through one thing, anxious to get on with the next. We spend precious time and energy cleaning up our own messes instead of applying ourselves to the task at hand.

Recovery from indispensability means that we get organized and stop using ourselves up on extraneous details. We focus on what's important, get far more accomplished, and feel better about what we've done.

AFFIRMATION:
Less is more.

The true reason why we know ourselves so little lies in the difficulty we find in standing at a proper distance from ourselves. . . .

—Amiel's Journal

Our indispensability keeps us from seeing the proverbial forest for the trees. Our clarity is clouded by always being in the thick of it.

We need to take a step back in order to get a good look at how we're doing. The proper distance is that which allows us to see our lives in perspective.

A day off or even a few moments in bed for journal-writing helps us to know ourselves better. If this seems like an impossible idea, that's the best reason to do it.

❋ AFFIRMATION:
When I stand back, I can see the bigger picture.

"Look here," I said, "people like to collect disasters."
—*Agatha Christie*, Endless Night

We chase fire engines or embroider our hardships in order to feel more alive. A temporary problem is magnified in the telling; the most trivial detail assumes greater importance than it deserves.

Being at the center of the storm is exciting and distracting. We have so much to do. We feel important. Disasters require emergency action, which immediately transforms the Indispensable Woman into Volunteer Firefighter.

Crises abound. What's more challenging is to cope without revving up the sirens.

✿ AFFIRMATION:
If I cultivate peace, I will be prepared for a real crisis should it come.

Secret: When you don't tell the truth about your needs to yourself and to others, you are pushing love out of your life.
                                              —*Barbara De Angelis*

We deny our needs because we're afraid they won't be met. That others will think less of us merely for voicing them. We pretend we don't need anything from anyone. And that's just what we end up getting: nothing.

We deserve so very much more. But we have to be willing to take the risk of stating what we need.

Step One is to be honest with ourselves: I am lonely . . . I need a good friend to talk to; I am scared . . . I need someone to hold and comfort me. Step Two—share these feelings with a trusted friend or lover.

❖ AFFIRMATION:
I need other people.

"I wonder," he said, "whether the stars are set alight in Heaven so that each one of us may find his own again. . . ."

—*Antoine de Saint-Exupery*

Christmas Eve . . . we turn our gaze toward heaven . . . a dazzling spectacle, the sky lit up with a million stars sparkling like a diamond tiara.

Tomorrow brings gifts and celebration. Tonight we affirm the miracle of life, giving thanks for the blessing of another wondrous year on earth.

Let it be peaceful, joyous, and may each of us find our star.

❀ AFFIRMATION:
Merry Christmas.

> *Who knows better how to push our buttons than family members? Who, besides family members, do we give such power?*
>
> —*Melody Beattie*

Our recovery is shakiest around family members. We're doing great, and then we go home for the holidays and turn into high-strung, depressed fourteen-year-olds looking for a fight.

It makes sense that in our family of origin we are the most vulnerable. That's where our dysfunctional patterns originated. That's where we learned to be indispensable. As a means of survival. A way to be loved. To be needed. To run away from the pain.

When we start to heal, the whole family system is threatened. Rather than putting our recovery at risk, distance may be necessary for a while. Until we are stronger. Until we can keep ourselves safe and sane.

❄ **AFFIRMATION**:
I love my family. I may not be able to be with them right now.

I have yet to hear a man ask for advice on how to combine marriage and a career.

—*Gloria Steinem*

My first take on this quotation was *"Yes!"* I'm sick of how men get to skip off to work, while women are constantly torn between keeping their marriage intact and building a career.

But when I really think about it, I wonder if this isn't an outdated stereotype. I know more and more couples working cooperatively, both struggling to balance the challenge of a family with the rigors of earning a living.

Maybe this is one time when we can learn something from men. Instead of resenting them for thinking they can have it all, we might assume we can have more than we think.

❀ AFFIRMATION:
Marriage and career aren't mutually exclusive as long as we are true helpmates.

I survived because I was tougher than anybody else.
                                        —Bette Davis

Just how tough do we have to be in order to make it in this world?

As we enter the twenty-first century, it's crucial that we feel free to express our femininity without jeopardizing our power. That we say good-bye to the era when women emulated men in order to get ahead.

Success doesn't rest on toughing it out or suppressing our softness. Everything we are—both the tough and the tender—can help us reach our goals.

✿ **AFFIRMATION:**
I don't have to fight to win.

> *All women hustle. Women watch faces, voices, gestures, moods.*
>
> —*Marge Piercy*

My daughter, Zoe, goes to a friend's birthday party. The other little girls skate merrily around the rink, giggling and snatching stickers from quarter machines.

Zoe stands at the railing, scrutinizing every facial expression and nuance, keenly aware of the relationship subtext. Has one little girl been left out? Are new alliances forming? Is there anyone who needs a partner or a hug?

She watches in order to know the score. An Indispensable Woman in the making, she knows she can never, for a moment, let up.

❀ AFFIRMATION:
I will occasionally close my eyes.

Vera said: "Why do you feel you have to turn everything into a story?"

So I told her why.

Because if I tell the story I get to control the version.
                                    —Nora Ephron, Heartburn

We like to have the first word. And the last word.

It's terribly important to validate our reality by re-hashing what's happened—in our words, in our way.

We want to be sure to create the right impression and not leave anything to chance.

In fact, we can't control other people's interpretations. Sometimes we have to settle for knowing what we know without convincing anyone of anything.

❈ AFFIRMATION:
I trust my own version of the truth. No one else needs to accept it.

Your best is truly enough.
                              —The Indispensable Woman

It may take our whole lives to believe it. That we need do no more than be honest, committed, and give from the heart with all the love and passion we can summon.

This is the task of adulthood: to believe in ourselves. To accept that our limitations are challenges to grow, to open doors to step through—at times to push through—after years of fighting the voices within that say we aren't good or lovable enough.

We are! It is up to us to repeat, each and every day, to ourselves:

❈ AFFIRMATION:
I am a truly worthy human being.

*Before I go up too far, I must go down deep into the earth,
to find the earth, and stay on it. I am in life. I am alive.*
                                                    —Anaïs Nin

No matter how high we soar, ultimately we must find
our grounding in the earth, in the center of our being.

When we know who we are and what matters
deeply, we no longer need to make ourselves indispensable. We love ourselves and let ourselves be
loved by those around us. We feel neither alienated
nor superior; we belong to the human race.

As we begin the new year, let it be with a prayer
and a song for how wonderful it is to be alive.

❈ AFFIRMATION:
Happy New Year.

INDEX

I would like to acknowledge the following books which were used as resource materials:

The Quotable Woman, Volumes One and Two, compiled and edited by Elaine Partnow, Pinnacle Books.

An Uncommon Scold, compiled and arranged by Abby Adams, Simon & Schuster.

Leo Rosten's Treasury of Jewish Quotations, McGraw-Hill.

The Portable Curmudgeon, compiled and edited by Jon Winokur, New American Library.

1,911 Best Things Anybody Ever Said, selected and compiled by Robert Byrne, Fawcett Columbine.

She Rises Like the Sun, edited by Janine Canan, The Crossing Press.

And Then She Said . . . compiled by J. D. Zahniser, Caillech Press.